A Grief Revealed

FINDING AND NAVIGATING *Your* WAY THROUGH LOSS

KAREN A MACE

First published by Ultimate World Publishing 2021
Copyright © 2021 Karen Mace

ISBN

Paperback: 978-1-922597-39-7
Ebook: 978-1-922597-40-3

Cover design: Ultimate World Publishing
Layout and typesetting: Ultimate World Publishing
Editor: Isabelle Russell
Drawings: Pen Beeston

Ultimate World Publishing
Diamond Creek,
Victoria Australia 3089
www.writeabook.com.au

Testimonials

'Disenfranchised grief in my life was a difficult issue to untangle. But thanks to Karen Mace, I have found a way to discover the hidden roots and process them to find health and healing for my emotions and spirit. She applies her expertise with rare gifts of insight and compassion.'

Dr Kay Job
M.A.(Theo), PhD

'The ways to find healing are complex and unique, but always handled with love, purpose and a calming reality by Karen Mace in her workshops, writings and counselling. Karen's skills to assist others to process loss and then to learn how to rebuild, recalibrate, and reach a new equilibrium are outstanding and give one the courage to continue on. Karen's abilities to guide individuals through the stages of healing, to renew hope and re-energise, are especially beneficial to again join the links in the chain of wellbeing.'

Thérèse von Samorzewski OAM

'Karen Mace is a talented counsellor, writer and mentor. She has personally travelled the journey of recovery from devastating grief and has a God-given gift of leading others on the same journey. Karen's wisdom, empathy and her ability to see straight to the heart of her clients have made a profound difference in the lives of many, particularly those who have felt lost, grieving in the abyss.'

Marnie Gadd

'I've had the privilege of knowing Karen as a colleague and a friend for some five years and know her as a woman of integrity, passion and compassion. Her own journey and studies have equipped her to sit with others, me included, and help us unpack the personal stories that lie within, waiting for a chance to be expressed, brought to life and understood.'

Dianne Hooley
Principal, Newstead Christian School

'I have known Karen in a professional/client capacity for four years and have attended some of her grief workshops where I was provided with valuable tools to be able to express my grief in a concrete form, providing perspective and ultimately experiencing emotional and spiritual healing. Karen's own journey with grief has enabled a compassionate and empathetic approach where that which appeared hopeless was now reframed with hope. I recommend this book to all who have experienced loss in any form as a valuable resource to begin their healing journey.'

Melanie Pearce

'If you find yourself lost in the wilderness of grief, then this is the guide for you. I can think of no-one more qualified than Karen Mace to curate these personal stories into treasured pages of meaning and hope. As a qualified psychotherapist, nurse, counsellor, educator and author, Karen has dedicated her life to helping others. But these paper credentials are not what qualifies Karen to help others through this wilderness; it is her own personal story of navigating grief that qualifies her. As one of the beneficiaries of her gentle wisdom and guidance, I commend this book to those seeking hope as they navigate their own story.'

Julie Sladden M D.

'As part of a Christian tertiary college's leadership team, I was relieved to have Karen as a person we could send staff and students to for counselling and direction. Karen brings a unique mix of medical, psychological, and spiritual insight to her practice. She draws on her own personal experiences of loss, grief, and restoration so her understanding is not mere theory. She is a wise woman and I trust this book will lead you through your own process of grieving as healthily as Karen has managed.'

Denise George

'There is a true saying that life's experiences can make you 'bitter or better'. We've known Karen Mace over many years and can testify that she has allowed her own experiences to bring life and love to hurting hearts and confused minds with discernment and prophetic insight, along with encouragement and sound advice to many. We ourselves have been blessed by her counsel and recommend her in every way.'

Richard & Anna Holloway

'I have known Karen for many years. I knew that she had experienced terrible loss in losing her two daughters, but I never really knew her personal story until recently after reconnecting and reading her memoir, *Healing Begins in the Heart*. Karen was the guest speaker for International Women's Day for our organisation New Mornings, she captivated an audience of women with her insight, stories, authenticity, and strength around the topic of grief and loss.

A Grief Revealed weaves its way around your heart and oftentimes I identified myself within the stories of others. The ability to support my internal tears through this book has been impactful. The realisation and awareness of what disenfranchised grief is and how it sits just below the surface of our lives potentially stealing our joy explained itself as I read through the pages. Associating grief without actual death was a new realisation. I have enjoyed reading Karen's work and the stories of hope and healing. *A Grief Revealed* is a read that will help unlock and heal areas that have been pushed below the surface of our lives. A very special book.'

Bronwyn Waterhouse,
Executive Officer, New Mornings

Contents

PART ONE

Introduction

My friend, Julie, and I were sitting at a cafe having lunch. Earlier in the year, we had committed to meeting together once a month to write. It was to keep us accountable, we said. So, there we were, meeting and eating and talking, not doing too much writing, but talking about writing and our work. I'm a counsellor, and I had been mulling over what I really wanted to specialise in as I was tired of trying to be all things to all people.

'I don't know what my thing is.'

'You don't know?' Julie chuckled, raising her eyebrows as she peered at me with a *'seriously?'* look on her face. 'I do.'

'You do?' I was surprised. 'What is it? What's my thing, then?'

'Grief. Grief's your thing.' There was certainty in her voice, and the way she sat back in her chair after making the declaration showed me she wasn't expecting an argument.

'Really? Grief?'

I pondered it for a bit, thinking back to the stories I had written, the novel I was working on, and the expressive writing workshops I loved to run. Grief was a common thread running through them all: loss, pain, sadness, resilience and overcoming; a walking through and with; sometimes alone, sometimes with others. I had to agree. Grief was—and still is—my thing.

Writing is my thing too, as is storytelling.

I didn't set out to write a book about grief. I was already busy working on a novel and working with my clients, so beginning another project went against all I was trying to do—reduce stress by reducing my workload! Then November came around. The anniversary of the death of my daughters, Sarah and Ileana, was upon us again. It's been almost thirty years since that horrific day in November 1993 when my world was turned upside down and pain like I had never experienced before bit into the very heart of me. Despite the passage of time, some years continue to be harder than others and, for some reason—I still don't understand why—November 2020 was especially hard. Perhaps because COVID-19 hit the world in 2020 and I saw the lives of many others turned upside down; perhaps something in me resonated with that. Whatever the reason, I noticed the grief that people weren't even aware they were carrying. Sometimes it hid behind depression or anxiety; sometimes it masked itself as frustration or anger or disappointment. Yet, if I prodded just a little, scratched the surface a tiny bit, the grief began to leak out.

The kind of grief I was seeing was what psychology calls disenfranchised grief. One writer, Thomas Attig, suggests the nature of this disenfranchisement is denial of the mourner's 'right to grieve'. Once settled with the idea that grief was my thing, I had no plans to do more than work with that, to continue doing what I had always done when I worked with clients—help them find what was behind their current pain, help them see it was okay to grieve. But, in November, the month our daughters died so many years ago, I decided I wanted to write about grief. At first it was to be a retelling of my story and my relationship with grief—and just for me. Because in the retelling of my life story, I knew I could change the way I related to my circumstances, to what had happened to me that had caused me to see myself as a victim for so long. I knew the power of my story and decided it was time to write another chapter of it.

Then, as I considered those I worked with, considered the pain they suffered and their attempts to hide it, as I reflected on each of their stories, I knew I wanted to write about their experiences of grief too. Many of them hadn't realised that what they were experiencing was grief because they associated grief with death and dying. I saw the bewilderment on their faces when I said to them, 'You're grieving.'

One young woman was quick to respond when I suggested she might not be depressed, but rather that she was deep in a state of grief.

'My doctor said I am depressed, and he's prescribed an antidepressant. Here,' she rummaged in her bag and pulled out a small box neatly labelled with her name and the details of the medication, 'I must be depressed.' She insisted I take it and note down what the doctor prescribed, frowning at me and biting her lip as I did. 'Why would I be grieving?'

'Tell me your story again,' I urged.

And as her story tumbled out, the tears fell. So much loss. Loss upon loss upon loss.

When C. S. Lewis's wife died, he told of how his grief was deep and overwhelming. He said, 'No one ever told me grief was like fear. I am not afraid, but the sensation is like being afraid.' The young woman recently diagnosed with depression told me of her deep fear that she wouldn't ever get past what had happened to her, that she would never be a wife or a mother because no one would want her if they knew how unworthy she was.

'Sometimes the fear is too much. I can't bear it.' She wrapped her arms around her middle and rocked a little.

There are several definitions of grief, but essentially it is a feeling of intense sorrow and sadness, the mental and emotional suffering and distress caused by loss and regret. By the end of our time together, the young woman acknowledged that she was grieving and agreed to work with me to find and navigate her path through the huge losses she had experienced.

Walking the path is not quick, and it's rarely easy. In fact, sometimes it feels like you need a machete to slash your way through; sometimes it's like you are walking through thick mud that wants to suck you down and it's all you can do to lift one foot at a time to take a step forward. I suggested to a lovely young woman that the path might, at times, seem a bit like navigating the fire swamp seen in the iconic movie, *A Princess Bride*. Although there are many dangers and obstacles on her path, the princess has someone who is journeying with her and helping her when she feels unable to help herself, or when she cannot see the danger. Even so, she still has to get through the swamp! She laughed and decided she would go home and watch the movie again.

'That's just what it feels like, but, yes, you're right. I'm not in this alone. Thanks for reminding me of that.'

This came from another young woman who didn't believe she had a valid reason to grieve. Because no one had died, and because she believed she had made bad choices, she blamed herself for where she now found herself. Blamed herself that a person whom she had hoped would love and cherish her had instead turned on her, abused and belittled her. When we talked about the lost possible self, the wife and mother in a safe, caring relationship that she had hoped for and dreamed of, tears dripped slowly onto her jeans-clad lap.

The grief work will be ongoing now that she has given herself permission to grieve. She will learn, as you will as you read this book, that grieving is not just about suffering. Through 'listening' to the stories I tell and doing the writing exercises I have suggested, if you choose to, you will learn that it is possible to experience devastation and suffering, yet reach through them to find hope, and in so doing, affirm life and a sense of purpose that pulls you through. Grieving is about both suffering and resilience. The stories you just read are what it's like for someone stuck in what we call 'disenfranchised grief'. Disenfranchised grief—the denial of a mourner's right to grieve— more than any other kind of grief attempts to bed the griever down in their suffering. They are also about a lost possible self, the loss of dreams and hopes that will never be realised. Throughout the book you will be provided with tools to help you navigate your own path through loss, as you face the grief in your life, or you can use them to help someone you know who is suffering right now. Because writing has been a powerful healing tool for me and for so many I have worked with, I have included an entire section about how writing works, along with several prompts you can use if you choose to allow writing to help you heal.

This book is not an academic treatment of grief. I'd like it to be a conversation with you. When I walk around the lovely, leafy village where I live, I often have conversations going on in my head, and with other people if they happen to be walking when I am. There's one person I walk with when we can manage to be out at the same time, and we often discuss the things I write about in this book. So, I'm inviting you to join the conversation. If you would like to add to it, feel free to do so by leaving a comment on my website: karenmace.com.

I am very grateful to those friends who have generously, and without hesitation, contributed their stories. They have made this a labour of love. I have changed the names and other details to ensure confidentiality except where I have been given express permission to use their first names, and all vignettes are composites of various stories I have heard over the years. Where grief is personified, some see it as he and some as she. I have not changed it to make it one or the other throughout the book as I believe it is important to honour how the writer perceives the personified Grief.

Chapter 1

Disenfranchised Grief

Although our world is full of suffering, it is full of the overcoming of it.

Helen Keller

When I talk about grief, the responses from clients usually reflect the way society sees grief. This encouraged me to explore the concept of grief and loss, and as I did, I became more and more aware of the number of people who don't feel they are allowed to grieve, or if they are, then there are certain rules around how sad you should be and how long you should grieve for. The term 'disenfranchised grief' kept popping up, so I attended a seminar with renowned professor Dr Ken Doka, who is attributed with having coined the term. By the end of the seminar, I knew that's what I needed to write about. This kind of grief describes any situation in which a person's loss is not being validated or acknowledged by those closest to them. Regrettably, it happens all too often.

After our daughters died, my husband and I came back from Ecuador to Tasmania. I noted the usual responses we received from people. Some who didn't know what to say said the oddest things; some, although not deliberately, said hurtful things; others simply avoided us. There was another group: those who were experiencing their own pain because of some loss, yet dismissed it or brushed it off saying, 'My pain is so insignificant in the face of what you are going through.'

Even while I struggled to stay in the world of the living in those early days, I knew what these people were saying wasn't right. I was so caught up in my own heartache I didn't want to engage with anyone really, but I had to disabuse these precious people of the myth that there are degrees of pain.

'Your pain is your pain,' I said, 'and there are no degrees of pain.'

One woman struggled when I said that.

'How can losing a relationship be as painful as losing two of your children?'

The compassion she expressed and the desire to comfort were strong. But despite the breakdown in her marriage, the acrimonious separation from her husband, the distress of her children, she insisted my pain merited attention, but hers didn't when compared with mine.

I've since connected with Tess again. This time, I was able to help her see the damage not validating her loss had done. Several years after the disruption to her life, Tess was grieving, but didn't realise she was. We talked about how, instead of allowing herself to grieve, she held onto the anger and resentment towards her ex-spouse and how this fuelled her interactions with him and how that flowed over into her relationship with her children. She told me how lonely she was, how she couldn't let go of what he had done to her and how she wanted to punish him. The only way she could do that was through the children. When I suggested we do some grief work, Tess agreed. She found little support from those close to her. She should have been over that years ago, they told her. Tess persevered despite the sadness, the confusion and the sense of isolation that seemed to intensify once she began to find her way through the big losses she had experienced. There is a freedom, a lightness, when we finally choose to acknowledge grief, to face it and the pain it brings, but from that moment, the beginning, the path is rarely an easy one.

In our society we are quick to judge, especially when we believe someone has broken the rules. Judgement shows up in many ways.

With sexual abuse so much in the news, it's important to talk about this once-taboo subject. Even though, in some cases at least, it is no longer hidden as more victims feel supported in speaking out about what they have been subjected to, there are many people who are decidedly uncomfortable about hearing of such matters and still prefer that it remains closeted away. But it's this very thinking that disenfranchises the victims of such abuse.

Jo was a lonely sixteen-year-old who longed for friends. At a school camp she headed off, alone again, to walk on a nearby beach. Part way along the path, a boy who had acknowledged her a few times joined her. She was grateful that he wanted to walk with her. Perhaps he would be a friend? Once at the beach they walked a bit and then sat down, hidden from the sea breeze by grasses and a small sand bank. Jo was feeling shyly happy to have this boy notice her. She wasn't prepared for what happened next and when he made aggressive moves towards her, she was shocked, unable to respond. Even when she told him to stop, he just laughed and continued. She withdrew into herself and waited for it to be over. Fighting just made him more aggressive.

Many years later, Jo was desperately unhappy and attempted to take her own life. Not long after, she was diagnosed with bipolar disorder. We met because Jo wanted help to manage the anxiety and the bipolar symptoms. As we talked, Jo revealed her story to me. It was the first time she had ever told anyone what happened. There was more that happened after the rape, more that Jo had pushed down, kept hidden, because it wasn't something you talked about. It wasn't acceptable. She was afraid of the responses she might get if she told anyone, afraid of the judgement, the condemnation, the blame. Jo was living in shame and the toxic, negative critic that inhabited her mind constantly reminded her of everything that was wrong with her.

Jo was never allowed to grieve the huge losses that happened when she was in her teens. So, her attempt to take her life was a call for help. I'm grateful we met and got to work together. Jo has always been a gifted, talented person with a wonderful personality and gentle heart. What happened to her in her past had robbed her of confidence in herself—of her sense of self. She tried so hard all her life to be someone others would like and want to know, when all the time she just had to allow her true self to shine through.

We've worked on many things together. Jo is growing into the woman she was always meant to be. She is bold and resilient after allowing herself to grieve, to be open about what happened to her, to work though forgiving those who tried to take everything from her. Jo is no longer listening to the lies about what is acceptable for her to reveal or conceal. She can't change the past, but she is allowing grief to take her on a journey to freedom, to a place where grief is no longer hidden but a part of who she is—in a good way.

While my husband, daughter and I were back in Australia after our girls died, I saw an elderly woman I'd met some years before when we were home, not long after Ileana was born. She was in her seventies. When she was in her early twenties, she gave birth to stillborn twins. As she hugged me, she whispered, 'Even now, without warning, I will be overcome with a sense of loss.' It wasn't something she could share with anyone, especially not close family. She tried—once—the rejection she experienced then remained with her. When the grief showed itself on those rare and random days, she grieved alone. 'The shower is a good place for tears,' she said, 'they mingle with the water as it flows away.'

'And then…?' I asked, even pleaded, 'then what?'

'Then I put on my everything is fine face and go out into the world again.'

My breath hitched as she placed gentle hands on my shoulders and kissed me on the forehead. Was that what it would be like for me?

Each person's grief is unique. The way we experience, process, and express our grief is different. You will see this in the stories you read later in this book; and in the characterisations of grief so poignantly written by the brave writers who wanted to contribute to this book so you would benefit. What works for me may be totally wrong for someone else. There is no timeline either. The woman who needed to go to the grave daily for two years did what she needed to do despite the constant advice from others telling her she should move on now, that there surely wasn't a need to visit her husband's grave every day. When we came back for good from Ecuador, I felt the need to go weekly to visit our girls, even though I knew they weren't there. Still, I went faithfully for almost a year. I know that caused raised eyebrows, and some even asked me why I wasn't 'over' it yet. We can't judge the degree of loss based on who or what is lost, what their relationship was, or how old the person was when they died. No matter the circumstances, your loss is real and the grief you feel is valid.

Disenfranchised grief is still very much a part of our world, but it shouldn't be. As mentioned earlier, psychologist Thomas Attig suggests the nature of disenfranchisement when it comes to grief is the denial of a mourner's right to grieve. In this book, I you permission to grieve what you want to, as you want to, without feeling guilty in any way. However, the reality is that those who don't expect you to grieve potentially won't understand your need for support as you process the loss. It's possible too, that the more you hear you shouldn't feel 'that sad', the more likely it is you will begin to wonder if what they say is true. And if you internalise the messages coming from others, you may well disenfranchise your own grief, you may well deny yourself the right to grieve. I have seen this many times in those I have worked with. What does that look like? You may find yourself experiencing doubt and guilt around your 'inappropriate' reaction, and ultimately instead of working through the distress, it becomes too hard, which in turn leads to difficulty coping with future losses.

You have a right to grieve the loss or losses that are part of your experience; grieve in a way and when and how you choose to, without the interference, no matter how well-meaning, of others. You have no obligation to grieve according to any rules set down by others. Others, rather than interfering in your journey, have an obligation to allow, to honour your right, and to refrain from being an obstacle in your experiences and efforts to navigate this path through the loss. What you need instead are those around you who support you, not alienate you; those who encourage you as you learn to carry the pain of missing those you have lost, even when those who are lost are possible selves and not those who have been present physically in your life.

Chapter 2

Lost Possible Self

To elaborate on loss, to look for some insight in it, is not just what a psychologically mature person does. It's how a person matures.

Dr Laura King

I first became familiar with the idea of the lost possible self when I started to use expressive writing in my own journey through loss. I had purchased a book, *The Writing Cure*, a book full of research about expressive writing. In it is some of the work of Dr Laura King, a researcher from the University of Missouri. I was interested in what she was doing and looked for more of her work. It was then I found an article she had published about 'lost and found possible selves'. That started me on my own journey of looking at my life to see whether there were any lost possible selves lurking about. There were. At this point in my grief journey, I had acknowledged that I was grieving, that I had a right to grieve, and that I needed to grieve. I was going around in circles though. Yes, our daughters had died, and of course I was grieving—finally—the loss of my precious girls, but there was something else and I didn't know what it was. I was becoming frustrated and that, in turn, was having a negative effect on my newly ignited faith in God.

Possible selves are defined as personalised representations of important life goals. Our lost possible selves then, are representations of unachieved, unaccomplished or now unattainable important life goals.

Stop for a moment and think about the term 'lost possible self.' What comes to mind for you? Dr Laura King's work related specifically to divorced women but I decided to apply the notion to myself. I used an expressive writing prompt called Clustering. It's a bit like brainstorming and is a journal technique that allows you to access lots of information very quickly. At first, I drew a circle, and in the circle, I wrote the words:

What never was
What almost was
What no longer is

and then I just let my mind run. Well, I had lines going every which way, with things I had never consciously considered, popping up all over the page. What would you write in the blank spaces? Try it and see what happens.

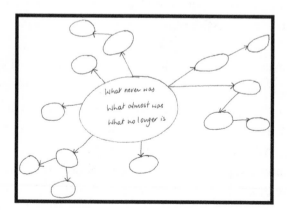

When we use this prompt in the writing workshops some people can fill an A4 page—or more! Sometimes all it takes is what you see above—place one word in each blank space and what needs to come out simply flows. When you have that 'aha!' moment, stop Clustering and simply write. Write until you run out of what needs to be expressed, or until you are exhausted. Your Cluster doesn't have to look like mine. You can choose to put just one of the statements at a time in the nucleus if you like. There is no right or wrong way to approach Clustering.

Sometime before this I did a course through the Center for Journal Therapy about writing through transitions. In the course we discussed writing about non-events—things that you anticipate that don't happen. I considered this as I journaled about what had come out of the clustering exercise. It seemed, in my case, lost possible selves and non-events were closely linked. For example, I had dreamed of Miriam, our eldest daughter, and Ileana and Sarah bringing their children home for Christmas sometime in the future and wondered what that would be like. It's only natural that we imagine such things and think about our role as mum and grandmother—and consider various scenarios with us and our future grown children playing our parts. But once Ileana and Sarah died, those dreams died with them, and so did the idea of me as mum to them as adults, and grandmother to their children. I had never considered that my grief journey would take me to this place.

There were many more lost possible selves that made themselves known as I continued searching. Their presence no longer served me. I needed to say goodbye to them; to let them go. The relationship with my sister would never be more than what it was when she died suddenly only two weeks after we saw each other again for the first time in over ten years; the relationship with my mother, who died in 1989, a week after an unrealised cerebral aneurysm ruptured, would never be more than it was when we said goodbye and I left for Ecuador in 1988. I had such high hopes for mending and growing a relationship with Mum and my sister. What of the lost possible selves there?

In my work as a grief therapist, the lost possible self looms large. The more you dwell on it, on what might have been, the less likely you are to be content and happy with your life now, and the less likely you are to be able to envision a future with hope. That's not to say you shouldn't think about the past, or about what might have been. On the contrary, being aware of the losses and sacrifices of our childhood and coming to a place of acceptance of our life as it has been, is part of our maturing, and is a significant part of navigating well the path through the losses we have encountered and will encounter.

Thinking about the lost possible self or selves can't help but make you aware of their presence. Then you may notice that they weigh on you, like carrying around a load. I noticed it when I started doing this work myself. The heaviness was there because I was carrying those lost possible selves with me wherever I went. Mostly they were quiet, stored away, but they would, at times, stir and make their presence felt. Usually, it would be just one of them that would get into my head. My thoughts would become what I call deceptive brain messages and the emotions attached to that thought would be uncomfortable even to the point of me becoming anxious, or close to panic.

A writing activity I like to give people once we embark on the grief journey is the Best Possible Future Self. When Alice came to me, she had barely sat down before she blurted out that she wasn't sure why she was there, and she thought she should just leave and not waste my time. I suggested we chat about what was going on in her life generally, that she tell me about herself and her family. She and her husband had been married for five years, they had two small children, the younger child being only ten months old. As she talked, Alice described a marriage where her husband was emotionally absent from her and the children.

'He is a great provider. He has a good job. He is good to us.'

PART TWO

STORIES OF GRIEF

Chapter 3

Sarah

I'd been arguing with my husband, wanting to run away from my children, feeling like not a single person could understand me and what I was and had been experiencing, so one Saturday, after reaching one of my lowest and most desperate moments, I left my house at about 10:30am and did not return until 6pm.

Completely overwhelmed with life and not quite sure if I could go on like this, I changed into my activewear thinking I would go for a run. I was too upset, so instead I went to an abandoned quarry near my home. I stood near the edge for a while and wondered what the kids and James's life might be like without me. Better, I thought. It wasn't really a moment of worthlessness like I had before but more of a 'I just want this to stop'.

I eventually moved back from the edge and found a grassy knoll to lie on. I stayed there for hours just looking at the sky, feeling immense pain and loss. Glimmers of reason came and went as I texted my husband back and forth. After a while I started to feel like I could get up but like I've had recently when retreating to bed, I couldn't move.

Eventually, it was hunger that made me move. I needed to eat so I went for some lunch in town, still feeling forlorn, lost and like I couldn't go home. An emotional hangover, maybe.

I felt like I needed to be in nature, alone, a good walk. The nearest one I could think of wasn't long enough and sure to be busy. The other one I could think of I had never attempted—a three to four hour hike up Mount Arthur. I thought, *I am in my active wear but otherwise unprepared, I probably shouldn't. Maybe I'll just walk an hour in and come back.*

I arrived at the carpark feeling really anxious and giving myself a thousand excuses not to go; to go home instead. I was struggling, still with the thought that there was something wrong with me for not wanting to go home and still feeling I had to escape. Even so, I started the walk. Immediately everything else fell away and I was captured by the beauty of the forest. The green floor and moss-covered rocks. The absolute silence. It was the perfect day, not too hot and not too cold. Sun creeping through the thick coverage occasionally.

I kept walking, steadily inclining. I could feel the distraction and just relief maybe. I passed stumps, massive fallen trees, mushrooms, and while I was feeling calm, I kept saying to myself, *okay, time to go back now,* but I couldn't. I got to a particular stump that just looked magical, I was quite surprised to find a fairy figurine sitting inside with a peep hole at the bottom. I thought of my children and how excited they would have been to see it and that they wouldn't have made it as far as I had walked at their age. I started to feel the motivation. I didn't want my children ever to feel like this, but I knew that by climbing this mountain, by stepping back from a ledge as I had earlier, they could too if ever they had to face it.

The climb started to get quite intense and physically my limits were being pushed. I kept checking my phone anxiously trying to guess how far to go but also worried I might get lost. I knew no one else was on the track nor would anyone begin the climb as late in the afternoon as I had. I kept stopping and taking in where I was, finding more mushrooms, moss, some kind of amazing snail and patterns in the trees. I started to feel… happy. I felt so happy being with myself. Just me. No children. I can't remember the last time I felt like that.

I noticed the landscape changing from the damp rainforest to a rockier, drier path. The plants changed and suddenly I registered how high I was. The climb kept getting more difficult and every now and again I would look ahead and think, *how am I going to climb that?* I knew I had to finish what I started though, I had come this far—I was going to reach the summit.

I was all alone, aware I was very high up on the mountain, sometimes a bit unsure if I was still on the path, sometimes accidentally stepping on wobbly rocks. I was feeling anxious and scared now, rather than calm. But I kept going. I was getting closer to the top and the climb was becoming even more difficult when what was like a sense of angry perseverance rose up in me. I've felt this before. This is me to a tee. Feeling like I'm breaking through a glass ceiling is what I thrive on and I began to feel a sense of self I thought was lost.

I will *make it to the top. I* can.

Once at the top the sheer height completely overwhelmed me. Red, puffed, and sweaty I perched myself on a rock at the summit and looked at the view. Low Head, Bridport, the rolling hills of Lilydale, Launceston, Great Lakes, Tamar River and down to the South. I could see it all. I had climbed this mountain on my own. I was remembering who I was. Strong, capable and supported (my brother and husband had messaged me at the top).

I can see this mountain from my house and a few weeks later, I look at it multiple times a day. I can't quite believe I was sitting on top of it. It's all of a sudden become this incredibly symbolic sight that shows me that I can do it; that I can be a mum and a wife and still be me. Yes, there are changes taking place in my life, and changes that have already happened. Climbing the mountain showed me that

I don't need to feel threatened by the changes. It showed me that I am still me, that I am strong, and I can adapt and grow in these new roles that I saw as only taking from me because they are giving to me too. When I look at the mountain, I remember that.

Chapter 4

Pen

This past year has been a tough one as I have had considerable complications with my health. This has led to a new and close relationship with grief.

At times, I felt like I was wading through thick mud or constantly pushing a large rock up a hill. I did not think that I would be embarking on a journey this significant in my thirties, but here I am. I like to think I am a calm person, although in reality, my calm is only surface level. I have anxiety that I think is just part of who I am, and it has always been there. I like to be seen as strong, and I don't like to think I need others, so I don't talk about my mental health—or my physical health—much. Though this time there was something just not right, and I knew I needed to talk to someone.

Throughout winter, there were days where I was so dizzy that I could not get out of bed; my feet and hands would go numb and no matter how warm I was or how much I moved there was no feeling in them. It started with numbness in between my toes. This seemed odd, so I

27

went to the doctor. An ultrasound was the first of what turned out to be many tests. The problem was the result of a previous injury I was told; the solution—steroid shots. Thankfully, I was already talking to a family member about the numbness. He questioned this current treatment, so I changed doctors. I distinctly remember saying to the doctor, 'I am just going to tell you everything that I am experiencing. Who knows they might be all connected?'

Boy, did I put my foot in it. I do not think I have ever had that many tests!

One day in particular really stands out. It was after a blood test and I was at work and unable to be reached by phone. Later in the morning, once I was able to check my phone, I saw missed calls and voicemails. I don't know if you've ever been in such a situation; when I pressed play to hear the message, it was the voice of my doctor saying, 'Good morning, please call me as soon as you get this message, there have been some alarming results from your blood test.'

I remember the blood draining from my face, my body went cold, and my hands were sweaty. *What does this mean?*

I was standing in a car park ready to drive back to the office with my colleague and told her that I had just had an urgent phone call from my doctor. I excused myself and called the doctor back. My tests had come back showing extremely low sodium, I had to head straight in and get some more tests and depending on the results we were looking at me going to the hospital immediately for treatment. *WHAT THE HECK?* I got off the phone and called my husband to let him know what was happening. On the way back to the office to get my car I kept trying to process what was happening, arranging different action plans in my head—*what does this mean, what is going to happen?* My colleague, a close friend, kept saying,

'I can't believe how calm you are. You're doing so well. I'm here if you need anything.'

To be honest, internally I was freaking out. I was trying to make sense of what was happening, and the potential seriousness of the situation, and what my next steps needed to be. Sporadically I would start crying, overwhelmed by what was happening, scared that it might by really serious. My tears would well up and overflow, then I would start trying to process again. This circled in my head all afternoon. This circular processing would be the pattern my grief would take over the months to come. I headed to the clinic to get some more tests done and then waited anxiously all afternoon for the results. The doctor called and said that there must have been a mix-up with the tests, mine had come back clear and normal. What a relief, but what an afternoon. Still no answers, though. Sitting in the unknown is stressful, I often felt lost and became agitated with people quickly.

The week after that incident, I was back to see the doctor. I remember the moment clearly. After many tests, my doctor said, 'If these next tests don't give us any answers, then we have to look at the neurological causes.'

Now, a couple of very close people to me in the medical industry had already questioned neurological causes. One in particular was multiple sclerosis (MS) but getting told this after a lot of testing was a low blow. Shock and disbelief took over my entire being. I walked out of the doctor's room, out into the car park, got into my car and just cried. What does this mean for me? How do I process this? How do I come to terms with a condition that is deteriorating? Will I end up in a wheelchair? There were so many questions and no way to answer them, only time will tell.

There are no words that help in a situation like this. You know when someone has lost a person close to them, or just been diagnosed with a horrible disease like cancer? You wonder, what can I say? What can I do to make this situation better for them and less awkward for me? Don't say anything, just be with them and sit with them in the grief. Someone to cry with and agree that the situation is crap, is the nicest and most comforting support I received. There is nothing to do or say to make the grief go away, no way to fix it all up and make it instantly better.

I am fortunate enough to have a great support network of family and friends. It was these people who sat with me in the muck while I waited for an appointment with a neurologist. There were some significant moments with people who simply came out of the woodwork as I started to share about the journey I had been on over the past few months. People who simply sat and cried with me and offered their time. This time of waiting was the most difficult. I had been told that it was likely that MS was the diagnosis, and that the neurologist would take me through the next steps. Now, anyone that knows me will know that I am not the type of person that ever sits still and just waits for things to happen. I need an action plan and I need to know all the likely outcomes of what it is happening.

Fortunately, I was put in contact with a beautiful lady who has been in this place of unknown and has MS. This connection was invaluable, connecting with someone who has experienced this unknown, lived through it and is still pushing on. Her wealth of knowledge impacted more than anything I found on the internet.

Throughout this waiting I was still in the cycle of feeling overwhelmed and processing, though now I had another step in it, researching. My mind never stopped processing what was happening. It was hard to ignore because there were the constant physical symptoms, numbness in extremities, headaches, vertigo, complete exhaustion. Then I would feel overwhelmed with grief and hopelessness, I would break down and cry a few times a day. When I finished crying, I would come to a point where I wanted to do something, so I would do more research. I wanted to be useful to myself. The question I constantly asked myself was, *what can I do now?* This cycle continued daily until, a year earlier than expected, I got a letter from the neurologist for an appointment. I told myself this could mean that it is really good news or really bad news. 'Brace yourself' became my mantra.

Finally, the day came for the neurologist appointment. I was riddled with anxiety, plagued by the what ifs and what are we going to dos.

I sat in that waiting room with my husband, sweaty palms, holding my breath and braced for impact. I don't remember much about seeing the neurologist. There were a lot of questions about my health and the symptoms I was experiencing. I do remember this sentence,

'We have your brain scans from six weeks ago and the ones from four years ago. Yes, you have white matter in your brain, but the same amount was present four years ago as well and nothing has changed, this is really good. You do not have MS.'

What? Have you ever had a moment where you feel like you are dreaming? This was one of those moments. I do not have MS. The neurologist talked about atypical migraines that affect the body beyond experiencing headaches, and he said this is likely what is happening. I was crying again as I walked out the door but crying with relief. There are still not a lot of answers to what is going on, and I still have the symptoms and questions. I still have the same cycle of grief, but it is not as prominent.

It was important for me throughout this time to give myself space to grieve in the moment and not hold it in. My past has been riddled with significant grief that I have kept hidden in a box inside my head, unwilling to open it for fear of the pain that lies within. There are times when these kinds of grief have exploded from me, and I have had to pick up the pieces. Sifting through the grief in my past, the things I have held onto or hoped would be different, has been extremely painful and hard. It was important, as I moved through this health journey, that I expressed what I was feeling and experiencing in the moment, or at least some time that day. I did not want to have another box of grief to manage and keep contained when a memory or feeling is triggered. I am by no means better or over it, but I have learned to accept that it will be a journey and a process rather than a destination with an ending.

Chapter 5

Linda

My daughter was the first granddaughter in both my parent's families. She was a pretty, lively child with long, fair hair, and was a favourite with the grandparents and with her brother. At 12 years of age, she became a Christian, giving her heart and all she was to the Lord and within six months she had lost all her hair, including eyebrows and body hair to the auto-immune disease, Alopecia Totalis. The next few years I walked with her through the specialist visits, comforted her through the soul-destroying cortisone injections, as well as ill-fitting wigs and the never-ending advice from well-meaning friends and relatives who wanted to know why we hadn't tried this cure or that.

My husband and I felt as though we had let her down, as though we hadn't done enough, especially when Google experts kept confusing Alopecia Totalis with Stress Alopecia and suggesting simple hair treatments. They didn't understand that 'Totalis' was actually the description of a disease and that her body was destroying the hair follicles as they grew. My daughter didn't want us to tell anyone, to explain, so I found solace in my prayer room and in my work as a teacher. For some reason she was more distressed to think others might believe that the hair loss meant she had cancer. So, I couldn't talk to anyone except my husband, but he was struggling too as we both tried to appear positive for her.

We tried to give her a normal life as a teenager, but she was wearing a wig by this and was always self-conscious about it. She wouldn't hug anyone, even family, because she was afraid the wig might lift. Slowly she began to withdraw from us and from her brothers. She became jealous of their 'normal' bodies and life stories. Now, my prayers and Christian belief became a barrier rather than connecting us even more deeply as I longed for them to do. 'Where was this loving God?' she demanded. None of the prayers were answered. So, where was He?

I didn't realise it at the time but looking back I see that I grieved for a daughter to go shopping, discuss fashion, and share feminine insights with. I wanted to help her pick her party dresses and chat about her boyfriends, just as all my friends were doing with their daughters. They only saw the pretty girl with a cute haircut who smiled nicely when they asked how she was. They didn't know she wore a wig to hide the baldness, what she went through to pretend she was just like everyone else.

I soon became the enemy. I had thick, healthy hair and I was a teacher. I had a career, a job, that kept me busy and was a blessing when my husband lost his job. When my daughter attempted to follow a journalistic career, she became so anxious because of her lack of confidence that she pulled out. It wasn't my fault, but it felt like I had somehow failed her again.

Over the last twenty years there have been so many ups and downs. My daughter moved away from home, first to one state then another believing it would be easier to study somewhere other than Tasmania. Instead, she used drugs, alcohol and relationships with various boyfriends to try and fill the emptiness and dull the pain. Then she was thrown out of her rental accommodation. I couldn't tell her grandmother, or our friends how much we were helping her because I was ashamed and wanted to protect her reputation.

Nights became a challenge. I found it hard to sleep because I was worrying about her. Every time a friend shared how proud they were of their daughter and their mother-daughter relationship I kept quiet. I didn't have that; my daughter had rejected me. The more we tried to help and protect her the further she withdrew from us until eventually I found we had nothing at all to talk about.

When she went into a relationship I saw as positive and affirming, one where she would be protected, I could finally sleep at night. But it was short-lived. He became abusive and she was soon alone again.

I never stopped longing for ways to connect with my daughter and when she needed a new hairpiece that was expensive, one that would need replacing every few years, helping her was an opportunity for us to continue to show her we loved her. When she bought this hairpiece, for a short time, she felt more comfortable because she could wear it all the time; she could swim in it and wash her hair like a normal person. I thought, hoped, it would be the beginning of a new start in our relationship.

LATER

As I write this, we are coming to the end of a year where COVID-19 has changed our world. Our daughter has been stuck in Brisbane, isolated at home. I had to stop writing for a while because one of those grief pins spiked me like a giant needle. A dark cloud of sadness rolled over me. This writing is uncovering all the memories of drunken rages when she would come to visit us for Christmas gatherings. She would pour out tears of frustration and anger... and we would try desperately to hide her state from her brothers and their partners. One time I was overcome, she was so drunk, I thought she would die in our lounge and I just couldn't be strong anymore; I broke down myself. My husband was so angry with her, I thought we wouldn't see her again.

Despite the immense pain, the overwhelming loss, I also know that when it is almost too bad to bear, Jesus is helping me. He is uncovering the hurts, and I'm starting to recognise them. My precious daughter has dealt with so many health afflictions, and each one is, for me, the sharp prick of a safety pin of grief for my poor child.

One day soon I'm going to be brave enough to deal with them and release her. I don't like what's in me when those grief pins stick me. I love my Saviour and I hide in his presence, but sometimes as a new pin hits home, the pain is real, and then I pray for his peace and seek out his promises and try to show others less fortunate the love they seek, because I can empathise with them. This Christmas, I had to deal with a brother and his younger wife telling me about their marvellous daughter and son, and all of their achievements. I was jealous and angry, and I don't want to be. I went to church and asked God to release me from those hurts.

I understand now that this grief I describe is continuous. There is no conclusion. However, with God's help, the grief journey and my daily faith journey will merge as I rely on his Word and promises for my family. I believe in miracles.

Chapter 6

Di

Permission to Grieve

I don't know how she knew, but she did. She always did. Always seemed to know just when to text, phone or pop round. She never minded if I didn't pick up or text back straight away. She understood. She understood because she had been on this journey herself, though that was her journey and this was mine. Even that she understood.

'She' was my grief midwife, a friend who drew closer to me when my dad died and helped me to birth the grief that had been growing in me over the previous year.

I'd lost close family before, but never someone as close as a parent, and not like this. On the other side of the world, my dad had had an operation to remove a cyst from his brain and it had gone wrong, horribly wrong. Something to do with machines failing during the op or something like that. To this day the details remain sketchy to me, through my own choice to remain ignorant, perhaps, or to insulate myself from the pain. Or perhaps it was just the recognition that details won't bring my dad back, won't change what happened, won't necessarily stop it from happening to someone else.

My dad. My stubborn, determined, 'can do', 'unkeepdownable' dad who could fix just about anything, became my dad who couldn't breathe on his own, never mind walk or feed himself. He couldn't fix anything, least of all himself.

For a year, he battled to regain strength and walk a few paces. He was even occasionally able to communicate a few words. But for every step forward that he fought for (and boy, did he fight), infection upon infection kept pulling him back ten paces until finally, almost a year after the operation, I got the call that it was time to come home and say goodbye. Dad had fought his last fight.

Circumstances cooperated to ensure I had the privilege of sitting alone with my dad in the hours before he died (though he died with many of his closest family around him). Though he was not a Christian and had in fact often been suspicious and repelled by 'religious folk', he was now my perfect audience. I played worship music, told him that in God's house there was a place, just for him, and that Jesus would come for him and when he did, Dad should go with him because Jesus is safe.

Dad died, the funeral happened, I flew back to my daily life on the other side of the world, and that's when the birthing pains of grief really began.

I would love to be able to describe them in detail but, well, I guess I'm more of a big picture person. Suffice it to say, there was anger, denial, guilt, depression, sorrow, all the expected emotions. Anger: at the surgeon, the nursing home, myself. Denial: in living so far away in a place not touched or visited by my dad, I could almost forget that he had died. Guilt: did I say enough, do enough, go home to visit enough? Did he know how much I loved him, how proud I was (and still am) of him, how so many of my strongest qualities I've inherited from him, that I was so grateful to be his daughter and for him to be my dad? Depression: more on that later. Sorrow: my dad had died.

Along with my grief midwife, I had grief counselling, something I would highly recommend.

The time of intense grief is really a blur, but somehow, I managed to keep going to work, doing things I had committed to do. Other times I couldn't be bothered to do anything, so I didn't. Sometimes I cried, but not all the time.

Then, about eighteen months after my dad had died, I woke up one morning and simply could not get out of bed. Physically, I was fine; emotionally, I was paralysed, anxious and exhausted. I phoned work to say I wouldn't be in due to sickness and then texted my line manager with a far more honest message. That morning, I got myself to the doctor, got some meds and met my line manager for a coffee. She is an amazing woman, acquainted with grief herself. Another grief midwife.

A note on the medication I was prescribed: I don't say this lightly. I had been experiencing other grief at the same time, as a serious relationship had ended just a month before my dad died. I felt I was drowning and became suicidal. The doctor rightly saw that I needed something to help me get a fresh perspective on my life to even be able to engage with the grief.

I was forced to confront the utter desolation of losing someone that I loved dearly, someone who had always seemed invincible. I was forced to accept that I wasn't okay, and that actually that was okay in itself, even good. I was forced to face how much my sense of self had been shaken by this loss. It sounds like a cliché, but I reached rock bottom and discovered that God was there, he had always been there, just waiting for me. Underneath were indeed the everlasting arms. On that day, unable to get out of bed, I had a fresh revelation that God loved me. He loved me in that moment of absolute weakness and vulnerability. He didn't need or want me to 'push through', 'get over it', 'move on' or 'suck it up'. He wanted me to just be. This truth, this knowledge was moving from my head, through my heart, into my knower.

It was a long journey but slowly, surely, I started to recover, by which I mean engage with my grief. Between the friends, the counselling, learning to be kind to myself and accept that it's okay to not be okay, to not be strong, to be physically afflicted through the emotional pain of grief, I started to embrace my new normal. Most of all, I think the most helpful thing was learning to grieve *my* loss *my* way. Sometimes I commemorate my dad's birthday and the day he died, but often I don't. I recently gave away the jumper of his that I had brought home to Australia to remember him. But he's never far from my thoughts; I remember him in the things he taught me, the security he gave me, the love he showed that gave me the courage to step into the unknown, many, many times.

Life will never be the same again, but I have adjusted to living without the physical presence of my dad. He's still there in my thoughts, in my own stubbornness, or determination (determination is surely stubbornness redeemed), and other qualities. I still miss him. He features often in my dreams.

My grief midwife would say to me, 'Don't grieve alone, but alone you must grieve.' Not all of my friends were able to sit with me in my grief. It was important for me to forgive them for this and release them from any expectations and not make up my own story about what this meant. This in no way meant they were less my friends than I had thought, or that in some way I was grieving 'incorrectly'. Grief is a very personal thing and I found that my grief stirred up in some friends their own grief that they had not/were not yet able to engage with.

Sometimes, I find grief can seep out in the strangest of ways. In 2020, there were many losses, both small and large, that were worthy of weeping over, but I was busy and some of them I had bottled up, only to be released in a disproportionate internal response to the death of a baby plover at work. Fortunately, I was able to feel my feelings and recognise that they were based on other things, not just the death of a baby bird.

Through my own journey of grief, I feel I have been equipped and empowered to be a grief midwife to others and count this an incredible privilege. It is a hard, and at times lonely, journey but one I am very thankful to have been led through.

Chapter 7

Amelia

The Box

I see it in my mind's eye. It follows me everywhere, never letting me stray far. I feel it behind me now. If I turn around, I know it will be there, waiting to see if I will pay it some attention. Mostly I don't, but I have come to accept that it will always be there.

What follows me is a little box, tied with a bow. It looks very much like it contains a gift or a treasure, but I know it doesn't. Even though it's mine, I don't really want it. I often wonder, *does everyone have a little box like this?*

I'm no longer afraid to pick it up, to look at it and examine its edges. Sometimes I even undo the bow and take a peek inside—but only if I have to. I'd rather not pick it up at all unless absolutely necessary. But I know it is good for me to do this occasionally. And somehow, this practice seems to stop the box from getting bigger than it should. I tried actively ignoring it for a while but discovered that strategy just makes it grow.

Then, when I'm not looking, and at often the most inopportune time, it explodes. Much like a jack-in-the-box. The contents are strewn everywhere for all to see. It takes time to gather the items and put them back in.

The weight of the box is surprising given its size. The contents vary, although two items remain constants: a blank piece of paper and a coin.

The blank piece of paper

On this paper I write the current form my grief is taking: the longing for more children; the pain of being around new babies; grief that my husband has never really seemed to understand at all (it bewilders him), and the loneliness I feel; and a variety of other narratives, mostly self-indulgent and entirely unhelpful but they need to be expressed nonetheless—otherwise they grow bigger. Somehow, by writing them on this (imaginary) blank piece of paper and putting them in the box, they lose their power, and I am able to move on. The next time I open the box, the paper is blank again.

I struggle to name a specific experience of grief because I find it so pervasive and it surprises me by popping up everywhere, often when I least expect it. The lost possible self is a constant theme: the 'me' who imagined I would have the career, while hubby would be the house husband (because that's what he said he wanted all those years ago). We would have four children and life would be peachy. But instead, my inner voice says: *give up your training and follow him overseas because his dream is to re-train* (he would've gone with or without me); *oh, and then give it all up again* (the new career I had carved from scratch) *because he now wants to move back home; and here, now run this business. Sure, you can keep practising as long as you keep doing the other stuff, running the house, running the business... and don't worry about that miscarriage... what do you mean you want more children? Let's not do more children, let's do breast cancer instead. But don't worry, your friend nearby will keep on popping out babies, so at least you'll be close to babies all the time.*

As you can see, it's messy.

The coin

The coin is marked with a word written in tiny print on the outside edge: longing. On each side is a different word: 'hope' on one side, 'regret' on the other. I know what they mean. Hope looks forward and points to the possibility that something is yet to be: that the story is not yet over, and the final chapter will tie all things together, so it makes sense.

On the other side, 'regret' looks backwards and reflects those things that might have been, the discordance between the 'dreamed-for' and the actual reality. It encompasses the things I wish I'd done, or think may've changed the situation that is my current reality. It comes with a hefty dose of guilt for the role I've played in the status quo. I know that 'regret' is the danger side, because there is an underlying 'if only' assumption that has a God-like quality to it:

'If I were God, I would've written a different script.'

I guess both sides of the coin point to a kind of bargaining that I still engage in. As I think about them, even now, there is a lump in my throat. But I am always eventually drawn back to the 'hope' side. Maybe, just maybe, God can make good this mess.

Romans 8:28 says that for those who love him, God causes all things to work together for good.

Chapter 8

Sarai

⟶————————————⟵

It starts before I open my eyes and doesn't stop until I'm asleep.

It's the worst in the between times, though, and nothing I do seems to make it easier. I go to sleep hoping I can get comfortable, praying I haven't overdone it. Trying not to think about tomorrow and what I have to achieve because I never know if I can. I hate feeling unreliable. I grieve my reliability daily.

I wake up and begin with a body scan. Not a meditative appreciation, not a calming exercise. A medical examination I conduct on myself, praying that today's a good day, praying it's not raining. God, how I used to love the rain.

I used to love a lot of things.

I want to say, dramatically, that I used to love myself. And I did, and I do again. But the years waxed long between those points. How can you love everything you never wanted to be? How can you love the flesh prison you live in when it betrays you daily? Hourly. When it strips you of every freedom and passion you have ever had and

47

leaves you alone in the dark, and you're not even hoping for it to get better anymore. You know there's only one way out. You know there's only six feet between you and getting some rest, some peace, some freedom. I just want to go home. Those proverbial six feet are so tempting sometimes that I ache with want.

Even things that shouldn't have changed did. I was active in church when I got sick, two years married, happy. Seemed like no one missed me as I slowly disappeared, my body cutting every tie with everyone. The last straw was someone saying my husband's sin caused my degenerative autoimmune disease, when no one, I repeat, no one could have adapted better, looked after me better, loved me more. He and my sister were my lifelines. I ask him almost every day, 'Are you sure you want a faulty wife? Don't you miss the active woman you married? This is not what you signed up for.'

It's not what I signed up for.

I did everything right. I started the degree God told me to do. I married the man God told me to. I went to the church God told me to go to. I was obedient for the first time in my life. I participated in the healing of my suicidal teenage years. Miracles kept me alive and got me through. And it changed me, made me want to be obedient, to live in His court, and find peace in Him. I was actively working to become the woman He created me to be. I prophesied, I danced in worship; I lived to be a living letter of love written to the world. I was so close.

So. Damn. Close.

I don't remember how it started. When did I know something was wrong? I look back and see symptoms and moments that all add up to my disabling, degenerative conditions. When did I give up? When did I accept that I wasn't getting out of this? I remember God telling me to live through it. I remember realising that meant I wasn't getting better. I remember. I don't remember when, I just remember feeling like I'd been beaten and abandoned in an alley somewhere, naked and broken. Raw. Everything felt raw. I was scared of being abandoned and desperate to get rid of everyone in my life. I was so scared of people not believing me, of saying, 'But you don't look sick,' or accusing me of not trying hard enough when I break my soul trying so hard just to keep going.

I will leave you first. You don't leave me.

I don't need anyone. I need to learn to be alone.

I don't want you. I don't want anyone who remembers her. The before me. I can't be compared to her. I can't be her. I lost so many people and I'm not sure how many left because I pushed or because they couldn't handle my illness. One friend even found my walking stick embarrassing. Goodbye, we will not be meeting again.

I remember fighting in vain to be seen, to be helped, to find what was actually wrong with me. The battle distracted me from my becoming. I didn't realise who I was until it was already me.

I remember sobbing because, after five years, a doctor wanted to run all the tests again. I remember the look of pity on his face, that it incited my fury and indignation, but it fell away in the face of the relief. I was seen again. I wasn't just a problem in the too hard basket. I was a person; I could do this. I could be again.

But too much had changed for me to be her. My husband couldn't be who he was before, either. He could never go back to church after the way they had just left us alone when prayer didn't work. When we were blamed for not having a miraculous healing. It's not cancer, where people know, understand, and stay. It's a nebulous, ill-defined thing. There are good days and bad days… are there even good days? Have my standards changed so much that being in enough pain to whimper only once or twice makes a day 'good'? How do you go back to 'normal' when getting the flu could kill you? Hell, I'm one infected cyst rupture in my abdomen away from encephalitis with my VP shunt (a VP shunt is a medical device used to treat fluid build-up in the brain), and my immune system is shot, so… I'd die.

I remember grieving that I may not be the one to euthanise myself—the ability to make the choice. Now, my death may come suddenly because of a random infection. I remember learning fear again.

But it all feels so surreally different from me now. I'm trapped in my traitorous body. I'm taking almost two hundred dollars of medication a week. I can't be all the things I should have been—all the obedient things I was becoming: a good wife, a good teacher, a woman of God who is virtuous, capable, and intelligent. All the things I thought God was telling me to be. I still wonder if I got it wrong. I was twenty-three years old when I discovered I was never going to dance again. I was never going to be a mother. I was never going to be able to teach in a classroom. I was never going to Israel or Peru or Egypt or Spain. Hell, the flight to New Zealand put me in a wheelchair when I was twenty-five. I couldn't even stand, just shake, and vomit from the pain. I wasn't just trapped in my body, I was landlocked. I was almost trapped in my home because leaving was a million risks, considerations, and pains that I had to navigate.

What would she say about this? The me before. What would she say about my life? My priorities? My passion? I don't know anymore.

The me now is beautiful, not aesthetically superior to her, but she is beautiful. The me now loves her pale skin and her smirking smile and blue eyes. She loves the softness of her skin and her curves. She loves her walking stick, that grants her more freedom (and can also be used to hit idiots with). The me before wouldn't have liked the stick. The me before was always passionate and inclusive, but she had no idea what it was like. She inserted herself into spaces I belong in now, but I didn't then. She would love that I'm a disability advocate. That I'm an author. That I'm still married to the man she picked. She loved him so naively, and I love him like he's part of who I am. I never knew a home on earth as I did the feel of him beside me. The me before would not understand who I am, would not know where to begin being this person's friend. Would she pity me? Be intimidated? Be proud?

There are a million reasons why I'm not her. I wouldn't have still been her now, anyway. I'm freer from expectations. I'm living the most unconventional life and I love it. I follow my heart and my priorities are so different. Being her feels like shoving myself back in a box that will never fit all of me again. I thought I longed to be her, but I realise that I don't. I don't want to go back. But I guess there's always going to be part of me that misses her. Part of me that wishes my way forward would have made sense to her, but it doesn't. It won't. It's not bad, just different, I guess.

It starts when I open my eyes and realise that being me isn't easy, but it has its own freedoms and privileges. It starts in the shower when I warm my aching muscles in preparation for the day. It starts as I close my eyes to sleep and know that today counted. I counted. I'm free to be who I am, not who I was supposed to be. Not everyone gets so lucky.

But her body is still the one I dream in.

I wonder what that says about me?

Chapter 9

Gretchen

———————◀

When I think about the loss of my potential self, the obvious point in life to look to would be my divorce. I was raised to think that marriage was forever, and I didn't doubt that for a minute. I knew that I would get married, raise children with my husband, enjoy my grandchildren with my husband, and I always assumed I would be heartbroken when I eventually buried my husband. A lifetime of love. So, when that didn't happen, it was a shock. I didn't know who I was anymore or what I was supposed to do with this new set of circumstances. But in reality, it started before that. I think this is something I have been struggling with for most of my life.

My college dreams didn't work out as I thought they would. I thought I would have the college experience everyone talks about-that I would make lifelong friends and look back on college as the best days of my life. Instead, I was roommates with an emotionally needy and controlling roommate during my freshman year, and my co-dependent self jumped to her rescue; I spent my four years of college not making friends in order to make her feel better about herself. I was miserable. I look back at my college years as some of the most wasted years of my life.

Even within my marriage, there was a point in time, very shortly after we got married, when I realised I had married the kind of guy I was supposed to marry instead of the kind of guy I wanted to marry. Rather than facing that and dealing with it, I shamed myself for even thinking it and I lived a lie for over twelve years.

Once I found the courage to live my truth and leave an unhealthy marriage, I was convinced I would finally be my real self. I dreamed of being an independent single mother, and in essence I worked hard at shifting my dreams over to a new storyboard. It was harder than I thought. I struggled with being alone in raising my kids, without someone to walk beside me and feel the same pain I felt and who loved my kids in the exact same way I did. I resented having to work so hard and not having as much time for my kids. I blamed myself for getting the divorce, but I never allowed myself to grieve. I didn't know that was an option.

Eventually I met someone and started building a new dream—of a marriage that was done right—there was the potential for a slightly different story, but one that ended the same. And this time I would be myself. Unfortunately, my husband did not like my real self, and he became abusive. Instead of living the newly formed blended family dream I had, I was living a nightmare. I was devastated that I had messed up again. And so, I stayed longer than I should have. I don't know what finally snapped in me that allowed me to walk out the door and never go back, but it was the hardest yet most freeing day of my life.

I'd love to say that I got my act together and am living my best self. I'm not. I'm so saddened by how my life has turned out. I feel cheated. But instead of anyone ever telling me I had permission to grieve, I was told to look on the bright side, and to make the next chapter the best chapter. I felt so much guilt about my regrets. I didn't recognise that I was grieving anything. I just thought I was feeling sorry for myself for mistakes I had made. I had brought it on myself. It wasn't something to grieve; it was something to learn from and move on.

Recently I realised that not only do I struggle with never having attained the self that I wanted, but I also don't think I ever truly learned who I wanted that to be. A combination of a legalistic schooling system and a tight knit religious community told me who I was; what my purpose was in life; who I should become and how my life should and shouldn't look. I'm a rule-follower and a people-pleaser, so I took those qualities to the extreme and I still have a hard time shaking them. The voices are still in my head constantly. I so wish that I had been allowed to explore who I was and who I wanted to become during my formative years.

I am now 45 years old and I still don't know who I am. I lived a marriage that was according to the plan set out for me. I lived a marriage that was according to what someone else demanded of me. I changed to please people and appease people. I changed out of guilt and shame and regret and a longing to be accepted.

I've come to see that the thing I grieve most is that I didn't have the opportunity for one reason or another to become *me* in my own way. It is a hard pattern to unlearn. I am sad about where my life has taken me, sad about where it hasn't taken me. I have regrets I can never undo. There are dreams I had that are gone—I cannot rebuild them. If I can't accept that it's okay to be really sad about that, then how am I going to move on? I don't know how to do it. But it's something worth fighting for, I think, and I'm willing to learn how.

Chapter 10

Maire

———————————

Every little girl dreams about living a fairytale life, the kind that starts with a handsome prince and ends with a happily ever after. When I was a little girl, I used to tell myself stories every night before I went to sleep. The kind of stories that were fairytales. There was always drama and climax, but the ending always resulted in perfect love.

When I lay in bed, I would pray to God asking him, 'Please don't let me die before I get married and have children.' To me life was about love, about being loved, about experiencing love and everything else came second.

I never thought I would experience the loss of my marriage and the grief that accompanied it. Those thoughts never entered my head. How can love involve risk? Surely if I worked hard enough, loved enough, gave myself enough, that would never happen to me. The deep swirling pools of grief with its numb darkness never seemed a threat to me.

I grew up in a loving home with parents who showed me what it was like to love another and that cemented in my mind the life I wanted. In my teenage years I wrote stories that brought to life the imaginings of how my life would be. I knew life could be hard, but I thought I had the strength to get through anything, to make anything work.

The first boy I met at sixteen didn't see love as I did. To him, it was a way of manipulating someone to get them to do what you wanted. He treated me in a way that wasn't good for me and broke my trust, leaving a small chink in my dream of what a loving relationship is like and leaving me a little disillusioned. Being my hopeful self, I soon put that aside, turned away the dark thoughts and looked again to a future of love and marriage.

Life progressed and along came more boys and then men who didn't fit the mould of what I hoped for, longed for. I was twenty-one when I met a man who showed me stability and what it meant to go after your dreams. I saw someone who could love me as I always wanted. I threw myself into the relationship and things moved quickly. From when he was little his dream was to have his own family, and a relationship built strongly on trust. Our dreams, our goals and what we wanted and hoped to achieve were similar. We felt there was no need to go slow since it all seemed perfect, and so eighteen months later we were married.

Marriage was definitely not what I had dreamed it would be. He was argumentative, fast, and expected me to be a housewife while working. We fought hard and loved hard; it was beautiful and raw as we got to know each other and started planning our lives together. He always said I was his rock, his muse—right up until the end of our relationship. In those first years our combined vision and future plans held us together in the tough times; we worked on houses went on overseas trips and involved ourselves in small businesses. There wasn't a still moment. Everything was fast, non-stop, and things seemed to fall into place.

Our first baby was beautiful; a delight and a joy that brought us closer and slowed our lives for a few months. It really felt like all I dreamed was falling into place. Within the first year we started another business that grew quickly and was very exciting for us both—at first. After the first year of business, he started to change. The changes were really slow at first, so slow that I barely noticed with a little child in tow. He started to work some nights. At first, he worked from home but soon he was staying at the new office to work. He became more critical of me, my appearance, my values. Money became a huge focus and as the cash rolled in, he began to make bigger and bigger purchases, eventually not even mentioning the huge spending to me. He partied more, drank more, started gambling. Everything was still moving so fast, at a pace that felt as though it might tear us apart at times. It was swim or sink in our relationship. Our conversations revolved around work and every time things got hard, we bought another house or started another project. These things got us excited and focused again but it was only a band-aid, and as the years passed the band-aid no longer worked.

After I had our second child, I decided to move more into our business to try and find a way to bring us back together. Occasionally we would have these raw connecting moments where we came together and dreamed again. After, we would run together for a week or two or a month and it would feel so good, so right. These were the things I dreamed about in a marriage—shared vision, love, growth. My marriage was my identity. Fulfilling him was my main goal and all I thought about.

Our lives were changing all the time as we drifted further apart. He was away more and more and there were many times I felt as though we would lose our relationship. The lies became worse as time went on. He lied to hide things and the web of deceit stretched even further. The business had taken over our family life and the man I thought I knew was very different.

Our third child was a huge surprise and his birth seemed to bring us all together. However, ten months after his birth we reached a place where we started to lose the final part of our relationship—our dreaming, our joint vision. The breakdown of our vision meant the start of the end of our relationship. I refused to believe after all this time this could be the end. I knew I needed to do everything to keep the relationship together. I never wanted to have regrets, things I wished I had tried. I wasn't ready to let go of my childhood dream. This desire caused me to say yes to things that I should not have. To allow abuse that should never have been allowed.

A year later, my husband walked out on us without any warning. He came back seven weeks later saying things would be different, and they were for a few weeks, a month even, then it was back to the same.

When he left, I felt something break within me. I felt grief sneaking, sliding, creeping in. Like a dark shadow it seeped into the edges of me, like a black jacket that I couldn't shake. I kept things light and happy on the outside, wanting to stay joyful for the children but inside, at night, when I was alone, grief would greet me. I wasn't ready for grief, so I put it to the back of my mind. I wasn't ready to let go. Letting go to me meant giving up and I never give up. To me, it felt as though letting go of our marriage meant letting go of myself. How could I operate without him? And yet the seed of doubt had been planted.

When my husband came back, I welcomed him home. When things came crashing back down the only difference was the touch of grief which started a very gentle thought within me, 'Can I keep doing this?' Over the next precious months, I allowed myself to cocoon away a section of my heart. It was as though I was subconsciously preparing myself for what was to come. I still refused to give up, I still kept going. I wanted no regrets but above all I still believed in the dream and I believed all my dreams would come true if I just kept trying.

During the next year the voice of friends who had known me for many years was important. Their gentle words reminded me of the person I once was. I couldn't see the difference within myself, so I allowed their words to wash over me. Slowly, gently, I felt myself starting to appear. I noticed the tension in the house, the eggshells, the abuse. I noticed the things that I had been dealing with on a daily basis. I noticed other relationships and how twisted our marriage really was. I truly believe this year was very important for me. I spent a lot of time in prayer, in meditation and I looked for quiet moments to reflect. Without realising it, I was finding myself in the midst of a relationship breakdown, of growing grief. Without that strength I discovered in finding who I was, I know I would never have had the courage for what was to come.

We all have our final moment, the one thing that we know we can't deal with, the thing that takes us to the edge. It is often a small thing and in my case it was. Our marriage was over, and I wanted out. It was as though I was walking through the fog and the light came on and the fog cleared. With the clearing of the fog, grief snuck in like an unwanted guest and yet subconsciously I welcomed it. Thinking back now, if grief had not started when it did a year earlier, I don't think I would have had the courage to leave. The burn of grief had begun the important process of revealing who I was.

For me, the relationship break down was like a death. I felt like he had died, and I guess with the extreme change in him, the man I knew had died. He had died in my mind and so I treated the grief as such. Viewing it in this way has helped my grief journey.

Recently, I have realised just how numb I was in that first year even though I felt free in every way. The real me was starting to emerge and it felt so wonderful! Those feelings masked the grief at the start. I remember sky diving and I felt nothing. I didn't notice the numbness at the time. The raw edge of emotion and ripping apart my very core from someone else was painful. I wonder if the numbness that grief brings is helpful to take the edge off that pain? Is that how it is meant to be? To feel such joy and freedom and such deep pain at the same time is truly a crazy phenomenon.

To me I was grieving the loss of my childhood dream, the loss of myself, the loss of my relationship and the realisation of what that meant for my children. The layers of that have taken courage to work through.

Chapter 11

Alison

Grief has been a part of my life in many different guises, through the death of loved ones, lost friendships, unsuccessful relationships, and a child never conceived, amongst other small and large forms of grief that make up most people's lives. However, a grief I never expected, and one which many people would relate to, is related to my career. At first, I wasn't aware that I was grieving. All I knew was that I was in the midst of a very dark depression that just would not let go, and the anxiety that almost crippled me at times was something I could not stop. Grief is, after all, about losing something or someone and we can often experience this in our careers.

About ten years ago I left my home and all I was comfortable with, to take up a dreamed of position in a new city and state. It was hard to leave family and friends, but my partner of seventeen years has always supported me, and he willingly left his career behind to join me in what was to be a career opportunity I was very excited about. We were both excited and agreed this was an opportunity for us both to have a lifestyle and way of living that we couldn't afford in the major city where we currently resided. Most importantly, the position I was to take up was a dream job, where I got to use all my expertise and passion to take on a new role in a well-known and respected organisation.

The first five years went very well. The success of what I was doing was being felt within the organisation and nationally. I loved working with my colleagues and formulated good friendships and my partner and I enjoyed living in our adopted city and state. Things were going well for us and while we missed family, the move had proven to be one of the best decisions we'd made.

But then things changed with a new management regime whose values I did not share. The change was rapid and instead of looking forward to each day, I began to dread it. Life became so painful that after a couple of years it was unbearable, and I started to realise that the dream job I had come to was no longer the same. In the third year of this new management, the successful program I had started was closed. I had to make a decision to stay in an environment that had become intolerable or to enter the unknown by leaving behind a job which I had, at the start, been truly happy in.

The grief I was feeling kept me bound to my job probably longer than I should've been. My dream had been shattered and taken away from me through none of my own doing and I had no control over the consequences of either the undoing of what had been nor what was to replace it. I was truly devastated by the loss of something I had put my heart and soul into—it was far more to me than just a job. Fiscal values began to dominate decision-making. I was angry and hurt and could not reconcile the decisions being made around me with the high values I had thought the organisation would always uphold no matter what.

For over a year I grappled with these feelings of distress, until the final straw when I was sabotaged by the system and people who were undermining my existence and finally, I could see that staying at this organisation was toxic and unhealthy for me. To stay, to survive there, meant that I would have to compromise myself and my values—something I was not prepared to do. So even though a future outside of this organisation was uncertain, I left. My partner and I had grown to love the city we had moved to, which we knew would continue to support us and nurture us, so we stayed.

The relief in letting go was immense—to let go of the grief of 'things that never came to be' and understanding that there were other possibilities for me and that I needed to surround myself with nurturing, not damaging people was an important lesson. There were more important things than the recognition of a position, a 'title of success,' or the association of success with a tangible outcome. There were those who were nurtured through the program now successful in their own careers all over the world; the true friendships I've made with my colleagues; the unwavering support of my partner who never stopped believing in me and was always there by my side, my friends and family and my counsellor who guided me to the truth.

By letting go of my grief of things lost, of things not realised, I was able to open up a side of myself that had been dominated by ambition and pride to allow other unrequited dreams to surface. It is still an ongoing journey being on the other side of my grief and even in writing this small piece there are pangs of sadness, as I remember those happy earlier years here… While I am glad to have left behind the pain of the last few years, it is only through this experience that the happiness I now receive is my own creation. Although born from the grief, it is something I can now (largely) control and can move forward with strength, courage, happiness, love and a sense of pride in myself, knowing that I have moved through this grief into a person I again recognise as me.

Chapter 12

Elizabeth

In 2012, my husband and I fell for a slick sales technique and purchased an interstate investment property, which, as it turns out, we could not afford. After the 2008 Global Financial Crisis, there was money around to rebuild and we were considered suitable for a loan and refinancing. Extra money was provided as a 'buffer' and a personal loan. These did not go well, with a large proportion soon disappearing into a scam.

There are too many reasons to go into here that lead to us taking out these loans. One day soon after it was all in place, I woke up to realise we had a loan of half a million dollars. It took my breath away then and still does. It was so unnecessary as only a few years before we were almost debt free and owned our own home. We thought we were making a clever and wise decision with this latest investment.

Things became very intense, and I started seeing the first of two counsellors and also a psychologist. Thankfully, and I believe providentially, one of my counsellors, had been through an almost identical experience. It was a great help to find someone who understood. My husband has been supportive and understanding all this time. He acknowledges I have felt it more deeply though.

For at least five years, I would wake up nearly every morning with feelings of fear, shame, or both. Fear, that a few more bad decisions or events out of our control—for instance, an economic collapse would cause us to lose everything financially or at the very least we'd be in an even worse place. The threat of becoming homeless was present as I was aware that women over fifty-five were the largest growing cohort of the homeless. Even though we managed to pay our mortgages, the fear was still there.

Eventually, I decided that even if I, or we, were living this way with unstable housing, God would still look after us. As He always did! That was a turning point for me, and homelessness didn't seem so scary then. Shame actually felt worse. I lived in fear that certain members of our family would find out what we had done—particularly that we had lost money to a scam—and declare how hopeless we were. I wouldn't cope with the shame and embarrassment. As it is, I think many family members know more than they let on and out of grace toward us have said very little.

Nearly a decade later, we have only been paying the interest-only loan on the investment property without making so much as a dent in the principal, nor has the property risen in value. In the meantime, we struggle to keep up with what feels to me like crippling mortgages and property costs.

Loss from investment decisions is not something you feel comfortable talking to others about. Although it is, for us, a crippling loss, it definitely falls into the disenfranchised grief category. It's so hard to acknowledge openly the bad choice we made, or choices really, all the while believing we were doing the best thing for us and our financial future. We were sure this investment would be just the thing to set us up for a comfortable retirement. But what happened instead is that the choice we made has robbed us of the future we dreamed of and hoped for. Yet, there are few people I can talk with about this and fewer still who 'get it' so there is no way I can publicly mourn this loss.

Some consequences of our decision are: financially we are fifteen to twenty years behind where we hoped to be; one of us will be working until we are seventy just to pay off the mortgage; we are in a very different place to many of our peers; and the most distressing thing—for me—is that we have to say 'no' to attending family gatherings that are outside our state because we simply do not have the funds to do it.

Looking back, like most people, I have had a few experiences of grief in my life, losing people I know and love, but feel like I have mostly coped well with these. My grief over our loans in 2012 has been at another level entirely. And this is not because I put money over people; my friends and family know that's not so.

I've noticed in my reading that as with any deep grief, the grief of financial loss brings with it feelings of confusion, anger, blame, guilt, embarrassment, preoccupation, denial, shock, withdrawal and helplessness—all emotions I have gone through in the past nine years. Even panic attacks. The emotions ebb and flow, with different ones more present at different times, although the others are always there, not far from the surface.

All these intense emotions have taken away from the calm, trusting person I thought I once was. Perhaps they have caused long term stress issues still to emerge in my mind and body?

We expect to sell the investment property within the next twelve months. It won't fix the problem. We most likely won't get enough for the property to cover the debt. But it's not only the money. Oh yes, money may relieve some stress—recently we received token compensation, through the Australian Financial Complaints Authority (AFCA), from the bank and investment company and although I'm grateful, it has made minimal difference financially and done little to change or mitigate the overall damage that has been done. Certainly, the extra helped with our budget, but the whole experience has left a mark on me; it feels like a scar on my soul.

All along I knew this was something bigger than money. The entire experience has brought to the surface the need for me to tell my story and to choose, now, to change it for the future. I don't have to continue to live in the wrong thinking that was one cause of our poor decision-making in the first place.

Several years ago, I facilitated a Careforce course and as part of a section on anger we named the area where we feel anger. I was surprised to find participants identified parts of the body like the hands, feet or neck.

I have given some thought to the bodily impact of grief. My financial grief has predominantly been in my head, as in my brain, and also my heart but my present financial grief and stress is not, and never has been, in my gut. Interestingly, I expect future grief over the loss of loved ones may be heart-wrenching, gut-wrenching, or both. I know it is felt in the gut, for after my mother's death in 2002, viewing her body alone at the funeral home, I involuntarily in the moment, put my arms around my seven months pregnant belly and implored her, *why did you have to leave me?*

During this financial distress, a work has been done in and by my brain. I have a different attitude now to money and finances. A more grown up one.

I have taken time to figure out my husband's and my financial patterns from childhood, even generationally. This has been a great help. I have learned and read up about money. I no longer beat myself up over what has happened. I realised I lived in denial for most of the last nine years; now I am facing up to my responsibilities. After a few attempts, I have instigated some steps found in *The Barefoot Investor* book by Scott Pape. It has been liberating.

Although I have a new financial freedom, I know I still have the most important part of the healing journey to finish—that will be letting go of resentment and grief and fully forgiving those involved, myself in particular! I hope to do this *very* soon, as it has all weighed on me too long.

Chapter 13

Mel

————————————

A Distant Dad

Every little girl needs the love of a father.

I wanted a dad who would sit me on his knee when I was little and read stories to me, who would tell me how much he loved me and that I was his special precious daughter. I wanted to be able to chat with him about my school day. To hear him say, 'Well done.' I wanted a dad who would teach me how to navigate life, a man with wisdom to impart. I wanted a dad who would be protective of me and tell my boyfriend that he better treat his little girl right.

I wanted a dad who was proud to walk his daughter down the aisle and make a speech that made me proud to call him 'Dad'. But no, none of this happened. *My* dad was distant. *My* dad spanked me when I did wrong, but never praised me when I did right. He was a dad who never sat and played Lego or dolls or farm animals with me.

I was the good girl because I so desperately wanted to please him. I wanted to be able to chat with him about anything but instead I avoided him. He harboured his own regrets and failures. Perhaps this was why he was too difficult to talk to. He got angry very easily and I didn't want to be a cause of that anger.

I put up walls, so many walls to protect my heart, and now it is so hard to take them down.

This is a letter I wrote to my dad just before he died. I never gave it to him, but it expressed how I felt.

Dear Dad,

Not sure how to start this letter. So proud of the way you stood up for us (my brother and I) when we were babies and you chose to look after us and be our dad; that you chose not to put me in an orphanage despite the counsel of 'friends', but instead to look after us after Mum left you.

But when I was little you got so angry with me, apparently because I whined so much, and you hit me often.

I just wanted to know a father's love.

I wanted you to pick me up and hug me.

I wanted to hear you say you loved me.

I wanted you to sit on the floor and play with me.

I don't remember you ever doing any of those things. You were always so distant, in your own world even after you married again. If you were in the loungeroom reading the paper I wouldn't know what to say to you, how to talk to you. I would be sent to call you for dinner or lunch.

You never asked me how I was going. There was just an expectation that I would do well, and that I would be good. I was your 'good girl' but that wasn't who I was inside.

I remember coming home from camp at Beresford House after I had given my life to Jesus and being so excited and chatty and it not being reciprocated.

You never came to watch me play hockey. I would have loved you to cheer me on. I just always walked to the field by myself. You always seemed busy, but I am not sure what you did. You were good at fixing things like leaking taps.

As I got older you seemed to get angrier. You weren't home much. You left at 8 am and would not return till after 6 pm. We would eat dinner wondering what to talk about. It was usually about people from your work. I never remember sharing my day. I may have, but it is not a memory I have. Then you would not want to miss the 7 pm news on TV so dinner would need to be cleared away and dishes done by then. Then you would watch TV all evening till I went to bed.

I never remember you reading to me. That would have been so great to sit on your lap and hear a story.

I know this letter is quite fragmented: I think it reflects our relationship. I don't seem to have any significant really happy memories with you. I didn't want to stand in your way, or you would get crabby with me. I felt I couldn't enter your world.

I know life was hard for you and you tried your best, but still I often felt unloved and in the way. When I asked your permission to go somewhere you would say, 'What did your mother say?' You couldn't make a decision that felt like you were standing up for me, being strong for me.

I know you walked me down the aisle, but it isn't a strong memory for me.

I love you, Dad.

Chapter 14

If Grief Were A Person

◆————————————◆

The following are descriptions of Grief as a person because sometimes Grief feels like a companion, like a person who travels alongside us.

Grief, my unwelcome ever-present companion. Sometimes I don't even notice he is there, and yet he seems to always be lurking around, ready to ambush me at any moment. When he is quiet, I don't mind him. He throws his arm gently around my shoulders, not in a menacing way, but not in a comforting way either. More like a reminder that he is there, even if I can't see him. I have grown accustomed to the additional weight on my shoulders, accepted that he is a part of who I am, and that he will accompany me throughout my life. There are moments he whispers in my ear. His voice is low and monotone, barely breathing one-word reminders, just to make sure I don't get too far gone, just to ground me in my reality. I've learned to live with him in my life. I know how to navigate my days without his presence getting in the way too often. Every once in a while, I bump into him when I'm trying to manoeuvre through life, but it doesn't stop me, it just reminds me he is there. As if I could forget. *This* Grief I'm comfortable with. There are days when he steps right in front of me, arms crossed high on his chest, shoulders squared, jaw set, daring me to try to get around him. I can't help but stop in my tracks. And if I do, if I stop and look him in the eye for a time, eventually with a small nod of his head, he'll step aside, let me pass, and fall in step right beside me again. But there are also the dreaded times when he swells into someone towering over me, breathing down on me, and staring through me with his cold eyes. He's unpassable. I have no option but to cower on the ground, hands covering my head, and wait for the shadow of him to diminish. The weight of him over me is too much to stand up under, sometimes making it hard to breathe, but not letting up. Even when I beg him to just leave me alone, he doesn't flinch. There is no mercy there. And then, for no reason whatsoever, he fades back into my ever-present silent companion. I dread him. I fear him. I resent the weight he adds to my life. I am tired of him always being around.

Gretchen

I bind up wounds
    And I tear them open again without warning
    I soothe and heal
    I pick and prod
    I am the heaviest of burdens
    And the most refreshing of drinks
    Bittersweet
    I am unpredictable
    I am constant presence and never-ending absence

Concurrently
Always here, replacing what was
I am a gaping emptiness that can never be filled
When I arrive, I am an extrovert, loudly displaying myself for all to see
At first, I am welcomed
Expected
Appreciated
But after my initial introduction, I am an introvert
I am so shy that others may not even recognise me
They think I will go when life moves on
But once I visit, I never leave
I'm the awkward guest
So, I hide
A shameful friend
A private companion
I supposedly grow weaker in time
But that is a fallacy, for I never age
My strength lies in memory
In love
In loss
I am a master at camouflage
Until I demand recognition
I make myself known in the fiercest of storms
And in the stillest of nights
It can be comforting to lie with me
To look into my face from time to time
Acknowledge my companionship
Because I am a mirror that reflects a bygone era
A hollow where shadows dwell
Memories live on through me, so you cling to me tightly
Afraid to lose those moments forever
I replay lost times through rose-coloured glasses
And with brutal, jagged truth

I am the spouse you hate to love
But love me you do
You welcome me
For I prove love
Validate brokenness
Confirm humanity
I am Grief.

Jaimee Amelia Smith

Hello, Grief, my old friend
I've come to talk with you again...
Of a heart that is breaking
And a mind that is numbing
Bringing me to a place of silence

Hello, Grief, my old friend
I've come to talk with you again...
About a body that is always tired
About thoughts of battered confusion
Of a place of darkness and silence

Hello, Grief, my old friend
I've come to talk with you again...
Of the friends who keep on dying
Of friends who keep on leaving
Leaving me in the loneliness of silence

Hello, Grief, my old friend
I've come to talk with you again…
Of a place full of hate and anger
Of a place full of fear and mistrust
Alone in a darkened room of silence

Hello, Grief, my old friend
I've come to talk with you again…
Of darkened rooms with no windows
Of shouting voices with no sounds
Providing me with the sounds of silence

Hello, Grief, my old friend
I've come to talk with you again…
Of feelings of hopelessness
Of feelings of forgetfulness
Taking me to a mind of silence

Hello, Grief, my old friend
I've come to talk with you again…
About a life that is wasting
About a life that could be flying
Away from these sounds of silence.

Alison

When I used to consider grief, I imagined it as a thick, grey cloud enveloping, suffocating, and oppressing every fibre of my mind and being, like Mr Huff in the picture book of the same name by Anna Walker. Since engaging with my grief, I have come to see it as a dear friend who takes my hand to help me cross an eight-lane highway in rush hour. Grief is like someone I can be safe with and trust to lead me through the most challenging obstacles. Grief has taught me it can be trusted with my heart. More than that, in daring to open my heart to examine the grief within, grief has reflected to me the state of my heart. It has given me permission to weep with sorrow, cry tears of laughter and howl in frustration. Grief has shown me just how deeply I can love and be loved. Grief has shown me that while it may never leave me, it continuously morphs and shifts, teaches and grows me, increasing my capacity to give and receive love, empathy and compassion.

Amelia

Groaning inwardly, I recognise the familiar feeling of someone standing beside me. I don't need to look. I know it's you. You're my ever-present, unwelcome companion.

Removal of your presence, though desirable, is impossible. It would be less like removing a thorn, and more like removing a limb, or an annoying family member. It's just not going to happen. I know we will always be a part of each other's lives.

Intertwined as we are, you keep me honest about the true desires of my heart, and the longings for the life imagined. While I am honest, you remain understanding and supportive, providing a warm hug of acceptance as I crawl into your arms on bad days. But if I hide things from you, then your disapproval is felt as you prick me with painful memories and accusations.

Even though I wish I didn't know you, I've begun to appreciate the things you have taught me. I've learned the joy of small and precious moments, how to sit silently with someone in their grief, and how to have courage in my own. Without you by my side, teaching me, these lessons may never have been learned.

For every moment I have resented your presence, I can also appreciate how you have changed me... for the better. I no longer fight you, ignore you, or resent you. If it weren't for you, I would not be the person I am today. In some ways, your companionship is a gift. An unwelcome gift, but a gift nonetheless.

Di

Grief, you are always there like a dripping tap, constantly reminding me of things lost and things never born; always in the background as life moves on but never letting up, never giving me a break.

'Grief, go away!' I say, but instead the tears come as I'm reminded of some other disappointment. Tears flow until uncontrollable sobbing breaks loose.

Grief says, 'It's okay, I'm collecting all those tears, not one is wasted. The bottles are lining up and there are more to fill. And with each filled bottle comes healing, more healing.'

Grief is my friend, sometimes too close for comfort, but constantly in the background, fighting for time and space in my life to reveal truth. Ah, truth—thank you, Grief, because as I journey with you, truth is revealed—no more hiding you away but come, Grief, come do your work, because as truth is revealed, burdens are lifted, and freedom comes!

Mel

Grief has come to me through my life, with distinct faces, different forms. When I was a child, Grief was an angry face and tears of pain, fear, or frustration. As a teenager and young adult, grief morphed into a romantic figure of unrequited love in a life in which friendships changed, and emotional turbulence was a given in the quest to find oneself. Then, with frightening ease, Grief showed up as the Grim Reaper when my dad died unexpectedly. Although as a new Christian I believed in a loving God who had taken my dad into the safety of eternal life and grace, Grief became an unwelcome visitor, associated with death and the enemy's plan to bring sadness. And when my daughter began to walk her own grief journey, one of sickness and despair, I found my image of grief changed again.

Now, I see Grief as a ragged, faceless, menacing figure. He wears an oversized, dark coat with ragged tags hanging off the sleeves and a collar pierced through with rusty safety pins. The safety pins appear to represent dusty shadows of unknown emotional debris. They take me by surprise sometimes, those pins, and when they prod me with their sharp points, they hurt.

Linda

Moving through Grief

This drawing by artist, Pen Beeston, depicts her understanding of movement through a relationship with Grief. We go from being almost slain by it to a place of acceptance. This allows us to continue through life knowing Grief will pop in and out, but also knowing we are strong enough to handle whatever Grief wants to show us in those moments he or she makes an appearance.

PART THREE

TOOLS FOR THE JOURNEY

Chapter 15

The Power of Self-Care

Men ought to know that from the brain, and from the brain only, arise our pleasures, joys, laughter and jests, as well as our sorrows, pains, griefs and tears. Through it, in particular, we think, see, hear and distinguish the ugly from the beautiful, the bad from the good, the pleasant from the unpleasant. It is the same thing which makes us mad or delirious, inspires us with fear, brings sleeplessness and aimless anxieties... In these ways I hold that the brain is the most powerful organ in the human body.

Hippocrates

Grief is a powerful, multifaceted and uncontrollable response that we experience following a painful or traumatic event. It can completely consume you mentally, physically, emotionally and even spiritually—and it doesn't just happen with the traditional sense of loss, that is the death of someone loved, special and important in our life.

Most of the research around the effects of grief has to do with loss of a loved one through death, however loss in any form can have the same devastating effects as the death of someone close to us. Self-care involves some of what we'll talk about in other chapters—telling our story, staying connected to others, being kind to ourselves, which sometimes involves forgiving ourselves, and learning to 'lean in' to the variety of emotions that assail us as we grieve. However, there are also practical things we can do to care for ourselves and that's what I want to talk about here.

Whenever there is any major life change, expected or not, grieving will be a part of transitioning to the 'new normal'. The transition time, which is our psychological response to the change that is happening, can be bumpy and extremely uncomfortable, and it's often a time when self-care becomes the least of our priorities. However, considering how stressful this time is, self-care should be at the top of our list.

Normal grief rarely requires professional intervention. However, where there is disenfranchised grief, the stress that comes with pushing it down, or not acknowledging it becomes ongoing or chronic, and that's when we may need some help.

I've had clients come to me for help with depression and anxiety, only to find as we talked that at the heart of the problem was unacknowledged grief. Abby, mourning the loss of her father, was concerned there was something drastically wrong with her. I gave her a list of normal emotional, cognitive, behavioural and physical reactions and asked if she was experiencing any of them. As she read them, she placed a hand over her mouth and half-sobbed, half-laughed, and nodded constantly until she came to the end.

'So, all of this,' she waved the sheet of paper, 'all of this is… normal?'

When I nodded and agreed that, yes, it was absolutely normal for her to be experiencing those things, she let the paper flutter to the floor, covered her eyes and sobbed.

It was the first time she had cried, she said. She was exhausted from trying to be strong for her mum; she had taken only a couple of days off from work because they were short staffed, and she felt guilty taking the time. And because she wanted to spare her mum, and her brother was working overseas, it had fallen to her to arrange the funeral and let everyone know about her dad.

We put a plan in place for her, which was all about self-care, starting with taking time off from work. I gave her some journal prompts to help her begin processing what had happened, and she said she thought her mum would benefit from them too. She chose to be open with her mum about how she was feeling and, instead of distressing her mum, it drew them together, connecting them in a new way as they shared stories of her dad, and talked about how life would be for them without him. A big thing to work on for her was her eating. In just a short time, she had lost over five kilograms and struggled to eat.

It's not unusual when grieving to experience a disruption of our normal eating habits or routines. This should be temporary. After our girls died, I struggled to eat. Well-meaning folk tried to entice me, but I was queasy a lot of the time, had a hollow feeling in my stomach, and often felt nauseated. Abby and I discussed the importance of eating good quality food, even if it was in small portions. She needed energy to do the hard work that grief is, and eating poorly and not sleeping well, also a problem for Abby, are both causes of low energy levels and a constant feeling of fatigue.

When we grieve, we are much more prone to illness. The constant stress of dealing with a big loss reduces or suppresses the immune system, making us more susceptible to coming down with a cold or catching the flu. And it's known that a grieving person is more susceptible to illnesses involving the lungs, such as pneumonia.

There is no way to avoid or eliminate the physical effects you might experience after a loss. Grief, although challenging and painful, is a normal and necessary response to loss. Over time, throughout a normal grieving process, you will see a reduction of these physical effects. Even with disenfranchised grief, once you are aware and if you allow yourself to grieve, you will eventually notice a reduction in the painful, and often distressing physical symptoms.

The most important way to help yourself when grieving is to take care of yourself and your needs. Listen to your body. It knows what you need. Following are some practical things you can do to care for yourself.

1. Stay hydrated

Drink plenty of water—filtered if possible. If you are craving salt, add a pinch of Himalayan salt or sea salt to the water. Try to avoid too much tea or coffee as they will dehydrate rather than hydrate you and alternate these with herbal teas. Sometimes it's tempting to use alcohol to dull the pain. If you notice yourself wanting to do this, you need to seek help. It won't dull the pain; it will only make it worse. Alcohol increases gut permeability and is quite inflammatory, so it will make you feel worse, not better.

2. Exercise regularly

Even if you didn't exercise before the loss, try to get outside daily. Mindful activities, those that require your focus, may suit best. Try walking, jogging, swimming, gardening or cycling. Preferably exercise outside. Being in nature, getting out in the morning light is especially helpful for mood. In his book, *Spark*, Dr John Ratey establishes the benefits of exercise. Exercise influences the same chemicals as antidepressants do, and there are several studies included in his book that show how exercise lifts mood. James Blumenthal of Duke University concluded, after their *SMILE* study in 1999, that exercise was as effective as medication. That exercise changes brain chemistry enough to help depression is significant since the grieving brain is very similar to a depressed brain. Even a short walk in the open air can help you feel better. Standing in bare feet on the grass or the beach seems to help too.

3. Eat properly

Dr Julie Sladden, doctor of functional medicine, encourages aiming for a nourishing, low inflammation diet. This means avoiding takeaway fried foods and processed foods, and especially high sugar processed foods like cakes, biscuits and sweets. When we are stressed, the gut becomes more permeable and leakier and, with a poor diet, inflammation can become severe. An inflamed and leaky gut can lead to an inflamed brain, and this makes it harder to process the grief. Work out what is best for you, and if you need help, please ask for it.

Abby found, and I did too, that it can be difficult to have a regular sized meal even if you are feeling hungry. Aim for small meals with fresh vegetables and fruit, good sources of protein and healthy fats like meat, fish, eggs, olive oil, legumes, nuts and seeds. It was tempting to have a piece of toast with butter and marmalade, or a sandwich as I didn't feel like much else, but I knew I needed 'good' wholesome food. Having a husband and daughter to care for also made a difference for me as I had to prepare meals for them, so I simply ate a very small amount of what they had. If nausea is a problem, you can try herbal teas like ginger, lemon balm or peppermint to help settle the tummy.

4. Rest

Sleep can be a challenge, as grief typically disrupts our normal sleep patterns. I know I really struggled. We need seven to nine hours of sleep a night. It's necessary for healing, immune modulation, detoxification, memory processing and learning. Dr Julie suggests an Epsom or magnesium salts bath if you are sleeping poorly. If you don't have a bathtub, try a warm foot bath with Epsom or magnesium salts for fifteen to twenty minutes, or try magnesium gel or spray on the skin. Try to develop a regular routine and schedule. Go to bed at the same time each night, avoid screens for at least an hour before bed—don't have them in the bedroom with you unless it's absolutely necessary, and keep your bedroom dark. If you are a tea or coffee drinker, avoid these drinks for at least three hours before bed, or even longer as caffeine has a half- life of about five hours, meaning your brain is still feeling the effects of it for up to five hours after you have the drink. And if you wake during the night, don't lay there for hours on end. It's better to get up and do something. I usually make a cup of herbal tea and read or journal for a while until I feel sleepy.

As with all parts of navigating grief, an important key to self-care is kindness and self-compassion. Do what you can, with what you have, where you are at. And don't be hard on yourself if you slip up or can't manage things as you would like to. You can always start again tomorrow.

Chapter 16

The Power of Forgiveness

> ⟩————————————⟨

When unjustly hurt by another, we forgive when we overcome the resentment towards the offender, not by denying our right to the resentment, but instead trying to offer the wrongdoer compassion, benevolence, and love; as we give these, we as forgivers realise the offender does not necessarily have the right to such gifts.

J. North, *Wrongdoing and Forgiveness*

She asked me what she should do, but before she responded, the way she reared back and glared at me with horror alerted me to her aversion to my answer.

When Nicky came to me, she wanted to talk about her mother. She had been having unpleasant dreams and was finding herself increasingly frustrated and angry when she and her mother spoke on the phone. Nicky came to Tasmania to be with her boyfriend. They met on the mainland, where Nicky, from overseas, was studying at university. As Nicky poured out her story, my heart ached for a child who had always been the adult in the relationship, making sure both parents were okay and, in the process having her childhood stolen from her. And now she said, it was still happening. Even though she was on the other side of the world, her parents still needed her, needed the money she sent home because her father had not had a job for so long. And it was Nicky who had to make calls to sort out any health or other issues because her brothers didn't take any responsibility for their parents. Nicky's mother constantly demanded but never gave. Nicky couldn't remember her mother ever saying 'I love you' or ever thanking her for all she did to provide for her parents.

'Shouldn't it be the other way around?' Nicky asked, her breath hitching as tears began to fall, 'Shouldn't it be up to them to care for *me*? To care *about* me?'

I sat quietly, waiting. I knew there was more and wanted her to share when she was ready. After about five minutes, Nicky grabbed a handful of tissues from the box I keep handy, patted her eyes, swiped her cheeks, and blew her nose.

'I feel lost,' she whispered, 'like a part of me is lost.'

Gabor Maté, a Canadian psychologist, has written a fantastic book, *When the Body Says No,* in which he shares some amazing insights into how disease can be the body's way of saying no to what the mind cannot or will not acknowledge, and how we can heal. As Nicky told her story, I remembered something Maté says about how necessary a nourishing emotional connection is for a child, and in particular the quality of attunement. Attunement, he says, is a subtle process in which the parent is 'tuned in' to the child's emotional needs. This attunement can be absent for any number of reasons and when it is, the child may feel loved, but deep down does not feel appreciated for who they really are. The child learns to hide the side of them their parents consider unacceptable, presenting only the acceptable side. They repress the emotional responses that the parents reject, which eventually leads them to reject themselves for even having such responses.

This kind of emotional separation won't usually be recalled as the adult looks back on their childhood as it effects the child at an unconscious physiological level rather than at a conscious thought-feeling level. I've worked with many people who insist they had a great childhood, that their parents were wonderful. Yet, as we talked and as they shared their story, I usually began to put together a different story, one where the parents were physically present, but emotionally absent. Just like Nicky's parents. This emotional absence becomes 'entrenched as the biology of loss'.

As Nicky and I talked about this, it was like a light going on in a very dark room for her. She was relieved to finally get it out she said. Now she just wanted me to help her with some strategies for dealing with her mother. Should she just stop talking to her? Refuse to take the calls? Should she insist her brothers take over the responsibility for their parents' welfare?

I don't think Nicky was expecting me to suggest that forgiveness was among the number of options available to her regarding her mother. It was this that made her react so strongly.

I left Nicky to think about it. Forgiveness has to be a choice and the person who is doing the forgiving must be ready.

We met again over the next weeks. Nicky alternated between confusion, anger, resentment and questioning why she was doing this, but eventually, in the third session, Nicky told me she had forgiven her mother. She went on to say that she hadn't been prepared for the immense change that happened as a result. She realised it was only a beginning but already she noticed a difference in her attitude towards her mother, and patience she had not had before. Saying the words, 'I forgive my mother,' was the first step in the process of forgiveness. After that, Nicky found her way slowly through the grief of a lost childhood, and how that had impacted negatively on her relationships as an adult. She wasn't prepared, she said, for how such a simple, yet terrifyingly hard, thing to do could change her life for the better as it had. Nicky's enthusiasm for the benefit of forgiveness extended to her wanting to share with her siblings what had happened, to encourage them to do the same.

In chapter one I told you about Tess. Forgiveness had a big part to play in Tess's healing. It opened the way for her to go deeper into the healing process, to walk the path she found for herself. At first it was a very lonely and isolated journey. She needed to reach out to her children who had distanced themselves from the constantly angry mum she became after the divorce. They resisted for a long time but eventually when she didn't give up, when they saw that there was indeed a change in Tess, and it was good, they stepped towards her until finally they reached a place where they could hug each other, and Tess could sit with them face to face and ask their forgiveness. They are still working on building a strong relationship as they learn to trust each other, and Tess has encouraged the children to acknowledge their own grief. After all, she said, they not only lost a father when the divorce happened, they lost a mother too.

> Life is short. Kiss slowly, laugh insanely, love truly, and forgive quickly.
>
> Paulo Coelho

Why is there such resistance to forgiveness and can forgiveness help in grief?

I was telling my friend and her husband that I was going to spend the afternoon trying to write about forgiveness in a way people would understand. Her husband piped up with, 'That's easy. Don't do it! Don't forgive!'

Why are people usually so resistant to forgiveness? It's because forgiveness is a big concept. For many it's something you do if you are super spiritual or close to being sainted here on earth. Most of the regular people I speak to shake their heads dismissing the possibility that they are even capable of forgiveness. They don't believe it's possible to forgive when something is so horrible they can't bear to think about it.

Corrie Ten Boom was one who thought it impossible to forgive. Corrie's family was arrested by the Nazis for hiding Jews in their home and eventually she and her sister were sent to Ravensbrück concentration camp during World War II. Her sister, Betsie, died a horrible death there just days before Corrie was released in 1944. At a meeting in Germany where Corrie spoke of God's forgiveness, she was confronted after the meeting by a man who had been a guard in the camp, a man who played a key role in Betsie's death. He said he had become a Christian and knew God had forgiven him, but he wanted to hear it from Corrie—that she had forgiven him as well. You can imagine that Corrie was assailed with memories of the horrific time in the camp. She wrestled with the most difficult thing she had ever had to do. Her decision was based on the message that God's forgiveness has a prior condition: that we forgive those who have injured or hurt us.

Forgiveness is not an emotion. And it was the knowledge that forgiveness is an act of the will, a choice, a beginning, that caused Corrie to thrust out her hand. She said it was her trust in God and a desire to do as Jesus taught us to do, that allowed her to do it, to say the words. And even as she did, she felt the power of God's love flow through her to the man.

Doesn't forgiving mean I must condone or be okay with what has happened, or what's been said?

In grief, we often hold anger towards the cause of our pain. The thought of forgiving brings with it the thought that if we do forgive, we'll be letting them get away with what they've done or said; that we'll be condoning, ignoring, overlooking, or even pardoning someone's bad behaviour. Why would we want to do this when what we really want is to see them suffer as much as we do, or at least be punished in some way for what they've done. Too often, it feels like the person, persons, institutions or whatever has caused us harm doesn't deserve our forgiveness. And they probably don't. In choosing to forgive, Nicky in no way condoned or excused her mother's treatment of her, nor did Corrie Ten Boom condone or pardon the guard's behaviour.

The people who have hurt you most likely won't deserve forgiveness. Forgive them anyway.

If you choose to hold on to the anger it is probably not just making you feel bad, but it could also be stunting the entire grieving process. Desmond Tutu believes forgiveness may or may not be appropriated by the perpetrator, but it always liberates the victim. When we offer forgiveness, he says, it prevents us from being destroyed by a 'corrosive resentment'. While we don't like to admit it, hating or resenting another person can be satisfying and so forgiveness can be disrupting. If you choose the disruption though, there is a lot of evidence to say you will be able to get on with your life.

What do you do when the other person isn't available or doesn't want to deal with you?

It's not always going to be possible to say the words 'I forgive you' to the person or to ask a person for forgiveness. This is where writing can be a powerful aid in taking that significant step in the healing process. Where the other person is not available or isn't interested in hearing from you (see Maire's grief story, or Elizabeth's story of financial loss), writing about it can be helpful.

Asking for forgiveness.

Sometimes we are the ones who have caused hurt or harm, either intentionally or accidentally.

She stood in the cavernous entry way; a little dot overpowered by the size of the space. She was three. She and I had just had a shouting match.

Well, I had done the shouting while she stood there, lower lip trembling, wide blue eyes filling. She clasped her hands behind her back and moved away from my verbal assault, for that's what it was, and watched warily from a distance. It was the hiccupping catch of breath that did it. What had I done? I was the adult, yet I had become the child in this interaction. Ileana waited to see what I would do. The guilt and shame that swamped me was almost enough to take me to my knees. What should I do? A similar situation flashed across my mind. Only I was the child, and it was my mum who was shouting at me. We were in the kitchen. Then Illy scraped her foot on the floor, and I noticed the distance between us.

'Ask her to forgive you,' a whisper came out of nowhere.

Could I?

One of the hardest words to say is 'sorry'. And one of the hardest things to do is to ask for forgiveness, or to forgive when you have been hurt. The resistance is often strong.

'Will you forgive me, Illy?'

She cocked her head to one side, didn't take her eyes from my face, moved a little back and forth. It seemed forever.

'I don't sink so, Mummy.' She couldn't say 'th' yet.

'Can I hug you?'

She nodded—slightly.

It wasn't long after that day that I no longer heard the sounds of Ileana chatting to the balsa-wood toucan she loved as she pretended to read it a story or heard her assertive three-year-old voice seeking an answer to her 'why?' I remembered that day when I shouted because she was bothering me, when I shouted because I didn't know how else to relate to this child who seemed to demand too much of me. I remembered that day and I cringed. If I could have, I would have taken a whip to myself. I deserved to be punished. And I longed to hear her say, 'I forgive you, Mummy,' but knew I never would.

99

After Ileana and Sarah died, I struggled with all that I wanted to ask forgiveness for. I was constantly distressed to feel there was nothing I could do, and I believe it played a part in stunting the grieving process for me.

For thirteen years I resisted Grief, but she was always there, looking over my shoulder, whispering in my ear, 'You have to face it. I won't let up until you do.'

Submitting to Grief and the work she was demanding of me meant not only facing the pain of the loss of Sarah and Ileana, our daughters, but also the myriad other losses that peppered my past that I had pretended didn't matter. And wrapped up in those losses was a lot of hurt and pain that would require forgiveness on my part, including forgiving myself.

In 2012, I returned to Ecuador. I went because I felt compelled to return. Our grandson was there at the time and so I thought perhaps that was the reason I wanted to go back. It was in the last week I understood the real reason I was there. I'd been writing a lot, processing my feelings, and jotting down my impressions of things and the changes that had occurred in the years since we returned to Australia. It was after I visited Cecilia, the landlady of the apartment building we lived in, and the building where Ileana and Sarah died, that the anger flared in me, quickly followed by a pain like nothing I had felt since the night the girls died. I was almost overwhelmed by the power of the feelings that rocked me, so I started writing. It poured out of me; until then I had no idea how much I blamed Ecuador, the people, even God for what happened to our girls. I honestly thought I had let it all go, but I realised as I wrote that it was something else I had pushed down and refused to face. And there was something even deeper.

In the years after our girls died, many, many people came to me telling me how brave I was, how they looked up to me and how the strength of my faith was such an example to them. And every time I heard such things, I felt sick inside while on the outside I smiled and responded with what I knew was expected, 'It's God who makes it possible. He knows and He allowed it for a reason. I trust Him.' I walked away from those interactions feeling deep shame and guilt, but also resentment and anger—and I had no idea why I felt the latter two.

What I realised while in Ecuador was that I had not allowed myself to show anyone how I really felt; I had refused to grieve openly and in a way that would lead to healing and the ability to move forward because I was afraid of what people would think.

I had a choice then. I could hold onto the anger and unforgiveness, or I could let it go, I could forgive Ecuador, the people—and God. In his book, *Forgiveness is a Choice*, Robert Enright says forgiveness is a path to freedom. But saying the words is often only the beginning of a process of forgiveness. I chose, while in Ecuador, to say the words, and I did feel a great sense of freedom, but it was just the beginning of navigating the tricky path through all that surfaced once the lid was off! Because, as I've learned, the work of forgiveness is ongoing.

Being honest is so necessary! But we aren't good at being honest about our feelings. I have been reading a thoroughly enjoyable and humorous memoir of a Canadian exchange student who met and fell in love with a French man while in France. When he moved to Canada to be with her a situation arose that illustrates this so well. After spending a lovely Christmas Day with Laura's family, Franck was quiet and introspective the next day. Laura kept asking what was wrong and he insisted nothing was. After the usually affable and smiling Franck continued to be withdrawn and didn't seem to at all enjoy the outing they were on with Laura's sister and fiancé, Laura confronted him, accusing him of being all kinds of unpleasant person and ruining the whole day. Franck was horrified and she could see the shock register on his face. Franck explained that he was sad. Laura was still angry and insisted he should pretend to be happy. This confused Franck who was used to, as the French are, expressing his true feelings. The very idea of acting happy, of pretending, appalled him as he saw it as being dishonest. Laura's response was that in Canada people feel responsible for other people's happiness and so you never let anyone know if you are feeling unhappy, sad or anything other than fine. She insisted he had to act differently to how he was feeling.

Does that sound familiar? I realised when in Ecuador that for a very long time I had been acting differently to how I was feeling, and it had not been good for me in any way. It spared others, but it damaged me. *Ah.* More forgiveness, of those who inadvertently, or deliberately, caused me to hide how much pain I was in. And the realisation that I am not responsible for anyone else's happiness just as no one else but me is responsible for my happiness.

As much as I resisted, I knew if I were to forgive myself for wrongs and perceived wrongs, I had to face the pain and allow Grief to come alongside me, to journey with me through the losses I had begun to list.

The poet Dilruba Ahmed's poem, *Phase One*, is all about forgiving oneself. She writes about simple, ordinary things and deeply profound things and for each perceived wrong she carefully states, 'I forgive you.'

Now I read the poem, or listen to it, and know the wisdom of offering yourself the gift of forgiveness. But for too long it was much easier to beat myself up, to live with the guilt of never being enough as a parent and the shame of not measuring up as a Christian parent; to let it be there, pushed down, only to surface occasionally, and only when I wasn't driving myself hard enough with the distractions of work and career.

I learned that the greatest gift I could give myself and my precious child was to forgive myself. It was through writing that I did this using an expressive writing prompt from Pennebaker's *Writing to Heal Journal*. You will find a modified version of the prompt in a free downloadable workbook. The link is provided in the Resources section.

Chapter 17

The Power of Story

> There is no greater agony than bearing an untold story inside you.
>
> **Maya Angelou**

Once upon a time... these words trigger memories of cosy evenings sitting on Grandma's knee in front of a recently stoked fire radiating heat enough to flush my cheeks. I'm snuggled into a flannelette nightie, we've had the usual battle to get my hair into rags so it will be in tidy ringlets the next day, and Grandma and I are waiting for Grandpa's radio shows to finish. My four-year-old exuberance is hard to contain as I wait for the next instalment of the story or the beginning of a new one.

I don't remember seeing books when I lived with Grandma and Grandpa, but Grandma was great at telling stories—especially fairy tales. When I started school and learned to read, I gravitated to its small library and always had a book under my arm. The book couldn't replace Grandma's stories, so whatever book I had, learned to live alongside the spoken story. Later, when I went to live with Mum, I still read books. Although I don't remember Mum reading anything other than *True Confessions*, she always encouraged me to read. Any wonder I love reading and love to hear stories.

I loved my grandma. She will always be a huge part of my life story. When I was eighteen months old, Mum, having decided she wanted a life without the restraints of husband and children, left dad, dropped my sister off to an aunt in country Victoria and crossed Bass Strait in the little prop jet aircraft that travelled regularly to Wynyard in Tasmania from Essendon. She had me with her.

For the next few years, I lived with Grandma and Grandpa in Williamsford, a mining village on the rugged West Coast. Just like that, my life story changed. And it was to change yet again, and again as the years passed.

Our capacity to tell a story is a wonderful gift. We all have a story to tell and if I asked you to tell me yours, I'm sure there would be unexpected twists and turns, some good and some not so good. And if you did tell me your story, would it be the same as the one you tell yourself or would you carefully edit it in the telling? As you read the stories shared in this book, you'll see that they tell of transitioning from one thing to another; of change that is world changing, sometimes in a good way, and sometimes not. Their stories no longer tell of certainty, rather they tell of resilience and adaptability, being able to bend and weave with the demands of life. A resilience that may not have surfaced if it weren't for the hard things and the pain associated with those hard things.

That's the thing about our story; it reveals a lot about us. In his book, *Mindsight*, Dan Siegel, author and clinical professor of psychiatry, says that how we make sense of our past, how our minds have shaped our memories of the past to explain who we are in the present, tells a lot about what our childhood was like. As we tell our story, he says, if we can make sense of the tough times we've experienced, we are more likely to have a better idea of who we are now, more likely to be secure in who we are. And if we don't start out with one, we can even change our lives by developing a 'coherent narrative'—a story that tells of both positive and negative experiences and weaves it all together in a way that makes sense. Siegel goes so far as to say that having difficult experiences early in life is less important than whether we've found a way to make sense of how those experiences affected us.

Writing is how I began to weave together a coherent story of my life. I wrote it and rewrote it; at first a piece here, then a piece there, so for a while it looked like a huge puzzle waiting for the next piece to complete it. As much as I knew I needed to get my story out, I also knew it was going to take me back to some things I didn't want to remember. What I didn't know was that as I wrote, things that I had pushed deep, deep down inside would make their way to the surface and demand my attention. Getting to the writing was constantly a battle; resistance was strong. It took a while for me to be honest enough to write it in the form it needed to be in to set me on the road to healing. I remember one day as I wrote, the memories caused such anger to rise up in me that my pen tore the page I was attempting to put the words on. Before that day, I had no idea the anger was so fierce.

In the expressive writing workshop, *Grieving Your Way,* my purpose is to give participants the opportunity to explore the difficult things that have happened in their lives, to acknowledge the loss and pain, and to begin to develop their own 'coherent narrative'—one that will transform their lives. I ask them to take risks as we work through the writing, as they begin to write their story, risks with their reality, their pain, and their emotions. To do that, you need to feel safe, and in the room on the days the workshop is held there is a sense of holding each other, of allowing, without judgement, each one to do the work in whatever way they need to do it. I notice as I stay close to them, that, just like me, the brave and vulnerable women and men willingly push through the pain, even when resistance is strong. They come to do the work, and most of them do choose to take the risks I ask of them, for some it is the bravest thing they have done so far.

When we start on our story, it is usually dysfunctional! That's to be expected. Initially, I found I was writing a lot of negative things; those were the memories that kept popping up, and those were the ones that brought up the anger and other unpleasant emotions. But story is one of the most universal and memorable ways we have of expressing what has happened, what is happening to us or in us, or what we expect, or hope might happen. And if we persevere, if we allow the difficult emotions to be there rather than try to fight them off or hide them—or run from them, that's when the story we need to tell will unfold; that's when we begin to make sense of our experience.

Earlier, I mentioned my journey as a toddler, from one state to another; how my mother abandoned me. Although I couldn't have been left with a more wonderful person than Grandma, still, it was abandonment, and there began the shattering of a storyline that commenced for me at conception. The more I learned about story, the more I realised that untold stories don't go away. We can survive the unexpected, the traumatic, the challenging or unwelcome things that happen to us, but if we try to keep the story from being revealed it will come out. It will come out in volatile emotions, or flashbacks and anxiety, in depression and in behaviours we don't understand ourselves because they are destructive. I remember the times I lashed out. The anger and frustration that was always close to the surface. The shame and guilt I felt after each outburst, after each hurtful, harsh word I flung at my husband or my children. The untold stories can cause ruptures in relationships, and mine very nearly did. They can cause a spiritual crisis, as mine did. It was in the writing of my story that truth was revealed, and healing began. It was in telling my story that I found freedom and the courage to say goodbye to some lost possible selves that had dogged me for so long. And it was in telling my story that my relationship with God began to flourish, that my faith became what I had always hoped it would be: connection and relationship with a heavenly Father. It was in the writing of my story that I finally allowed myself to grieve the many losses that were part of my life.

Author Jim Loehr says that our story is our life. He is right. Our life is full of stories combined into one overarching narrative. We are constantly telling ourselves stories about what is happening. Like the young man I was chatting with at a dinner a few years ago. He was quite open about what was happening in his life and as we progressed through the main course, I had to stop him. I asked if he saw his life as a story and if he did, what kind of story would it be. He paused, fork halfway to his mouth, glanced at me with eyebrows raised, then stated firmly that it would have to be a horror story. I managed to stop myself from chuckling at how serious he was. When I quietly suggested he was living as a victim in his life story, and if he wanted to, he could change his story to one of empowerment, one of agency, he almost choked on the chicken he was eating. To do that he would have to stop relying on marijuana to help him feel better, be willing to lean into his problems rather than avoid them and take responsibility for himself and his choices rather than blame circumstances or others for everything that happened in his life.

It may have been because we were in a public place and he didn't feel he could be totally honest in what he said to me, but he somewhat reluctantly accepted it, agreeing to at least think about our conversation. I noticed resistance as even in saying that he quickly added that if a person he was very close to didn't cooperate, he doubted things would change. The victim was strong, and it wasn't about to take responsibility for any change. He would need help to change his thinking, to begin to rewrite his story from that point on, but would he do it? I wasn't confident he would.

In chapter one I told you about Tess. For many years, her story was one of being a victim. The words she used to talk about her situation, her thinking, everything about her shouted 'victim'. Eventually all of this was subsumed into her very being, so her identity became that of 'victim.' It took time, but Tess did choose the better way. She chose life; an empowered, resilient life and willingly did the work to step on to and continue along the path to a best possible self. I hope I see the young man again one day, and when I do, I hope he tells me that the reflection went further and, like Tess, led him to make changes towards him becoming his best possible self.

Awareness is great, yet awareness without action has little value. If awareness doesn't cause us to lean into our problems with an open heart and open eyes then we are likely to remain in a place of suffering, even resistance. It's when we combine awareness and compassion that we get emotional relief, suggests psychologist Christopher Germer.

It's always a joy for me when I meet someone who is willing to lean into their problems, who takes responsibility for their story. When they do this, they learn to develop a new relationship with their thoughts and feelings rather than challenging them, and they learn to be kind to themselves. Like Susie.

I had spent a day at the local library to do some uninterrupted writing and had taken a break. My green tea was cooling a little, and I was leafing through a magazine. Out of the corner of my eye, I noticed movement. Then there was a light thump as something landed on the table.

'Sorry, didn't mean to interrupt you.'

She was mopping up her spilled coffee, trying to push it away from a novel that was definitely at risk of saturation. I passed her my napkin as hers was already shredded.

'Not interrupting,' I smiled at her, as Jodie dashed over with another coffee for her and quickly swished a cloth over the spreading mess. I turned back to the magazine and took a sip of my tea. I was thinking about a particular scene in the next chapter of my book.

'Do you come here much? I don't think I've seen you before,' she peered at me over the rim of her coffee mug. 'I'm Susie,' she cocked her head and waited.

'Karen. And no, I don't come often.'

108

My short break turned into nearly an hour. We didn't ask, but Jodie refilled our cups for us at some stage. Susie's heart was broken when the person she had hoped would be her life partner attempted to take his life. She had lived through years of threats, years of drug-fuelled irrational behaviour, but it was this act that caused her to see she didn't have to allow his destructive behaviours to guide how she lived. She came to the library for rest and peace, she said. She loved to read but hadn't been allowed for ages, so today she was reading. Even being at the library felt odd. She hadn't been allowed to go anywhere without permission for ages.

It was a serendipitous meeting. I was there just at the right time, and Susie was open to leaning into her problems. She asked for help and I was willing to give it. She is writing her story now, and as she writes it I hope to see how she changes the story she has been telling herself about not deserving better, about her partner's behaviour being her fault. I hope, after exploring her past, and beginning to make sense of it, she will write of a best possible future self. Alongside her story, she is also writing a goodbye letter to the happy and cherished self she saw herself becoming in the now finished relationship.

As Susie told me about her heartache, I suggested she allow herself to grieve; to grieve the lost dreams, the lost relationship, the losses that she listed without knowing as she talked to me. She was startled when I mentioned grief. 'But he didn't die,' she said. 'Grief isn't limited to death,' I told her, encouraging her to allow herself to grieve even though those around her were commending her for leaving what was a toxic relationship. In letting go of this relationship Susie set herself free to be a happy and cherished self, but not with the person she gave so many chances to over the past years.

There's a space that lies between what we have and what we dreamed of, between our hopes and reality. Educator and author, Parker Palmer, termed it the 'tragic gap'. This is a tough place to be. It's like the swampy no-man's-land between where we've come from and where we're going, and it's a real balancing act to stand in this in-between place. We are all in the 'gap' at some time in our life. And once there, we have to learn to navigate out of it. Pulling our story together, making a 'coherent narrative' can help us do that.

And it seems that storytelling is now the stuff of research. Neuroscientist, Paul Zak, discovered through his research that well-told stories release the hormone oxytocin, the neurochemical that tells the brain it's safe to trust someone. Oxytocin plays a pivotal role in forging connections and creating empathy. As you write your story, making it coherent and clear; as you learn to tell it to others, you'll find you connect with people in a way you never have before. I found this when I was asked to tell my story. In one-on-one catch ups, in groups, in meetings, or in the form of a memoir, telling our story can be a powerful way of connecting to others. After *Healing Begins in the Heart* was published, I received emails and messages via Facebook and my website from people I didn't know, telling me that the book had changed their lives, that they felt I was writing to them. We connected even though we never met.

Storytelling is powerful.

You don't have to be a writer to write your story. Just start writing. Use the prompts at the end of this book or some of the resources I've listed for you. But do start because the grief you are experiencing now, the path you are walking, is part of your story; a story that is longing to be told. And it doesn't have to be more than five or ten minutes a day to start with. In my writing programme, *Your Brain on Paper*, some of the prompts can be done in a matter of minutes—unless you want to write for longer.

Chapter 18

The Power of Connection

————————————————

Our brains are wired for connection, but trauma rewires them for protection. That is why healthy relationships are difficult for wounded people.
Ryan North

It was the end-of-year school concert. Behind the faded burgundy velvet curtain, my classmates and I pushed and shoved each other, giggling nervously as we lined up across the stage of the Memorial Hall. We had practised for weeks, and this was it. We were ready to perform our dance. My red, yellow, and white striped skirt swung around my knees, the cotton 'Mexican' style blouse hung loosely on my slender ten-year-old body, and the large 'Mexican' hat was secured with a cord that tied tightly under my chin. Sister Alacoque insisted we all needed stage makeup, so I wore bright red lipstick and some of Mum's blue eyeshadow. I was excited. Mum said she would be there later as she didn't want to be hanging around while the nuns organised us all and made sure we were ready. My friend Theresa's mum helped me get ready. I peered into the crowd. There was no sign of Mum.

The concert was well and truly over; the hall door clanked shut as the last person exited. Mrs Hudson was about to bundle me into their car when Mum finally arrived. She had a taxi waiting, so she rushed me off, barely giving me time to shout a 'see you tomorrow' to Theresa.

Mum didn't need to tell me where she had been. She always smelled of beer and cigarette smoke when she'd been at the pub. Careful not to let Mum see, I covered my nose to block the smell. There was no need to ask why she hadn't made it to the concert. Mr Evans, the taxi driver, was a good talker and didn't need responses as he chatted away, asking about the concert, expressing disappointment that he hadn't been able to see his grandchildren 'prancing about the stage.' Neither Mum nor I spoke. Once at home, I got ready for bed and said goodnight to Mum, all the time longing for her to ask how the dance went, how the concert went—anything—but she didn't.

I'm sure Mum loved me. But I don't remember her ever saying she did. And there was no genuine connection between us, no emotional connection. I lived with Grandma and Grandpa from when I was eighteen months old until I was about seven. I was excited to go to live with Mum and my stepfather, but the reality was different to what I had expected. In the years with Grandma, I knew I was loved. Grandma often hugged me, sat me on her knee in the evenings and sang to me or told me stories. I thought that was what mothers did, and as I was going to live with my mother, I expected things would be the same. They weren't.

Connection is essential and significant in a person's life; significant for all of us, but especially for children, because how we connect as children impacts how we connect as adults. In this time of pandemic, one of the most devastating things has been the severing of meaningful connection through lockdowns. The increased suicide rates in

Australia apparently far outweigh the number of deaths caused by the COVID-19 virus.

Deep personal loss throws us into a sense of disconnection that is hard to understand. Whether it is the death of a loved one, the loss of a spouse or partner to divorce, the loss of health or even the loss of a career that meant so much to us, our world as we have known it, and hoped for it to be, turns upside down. Such loss can separate us from the life and relationships we knew that defined our world.

For a few years now, researchers have been constantly finding new information about how the brain works which is significant for us and how we live. When I was studying psychology, we learned a lot about social connection and how this drive to connect with others and be a part of something bigger than ourselves is embedded in our biology. We are 'wired to connect'. In my case, in the situation above, I needed to know Mum loved me and cared for me. Her physical presence was not enough—and there were many times she wasn't there physically either. Unlike the memories of my time with Grandma, the memories I have of life with Mum don't include stories, or cuddles on her lap, and I don't remember Mum ever looking me in the eye and telling me she loved me.

There are specific networks in the brain that promote connection. One of those pathways is the neural pathway that processes physical pain; it also processes social pain. When we are suffering great pain because of a loss we experience, our brain interprets it in the same way it interprets physical pain. If you were to take paracetamol, apparently, it would reduce the anguish you feel because of your loss. But we all know paracetamol can't take away the pain permanently.

Before I knew Ileana and Sarah had died, I was working in the kitchen preparing the meal we were to share with friends that night. There was a moment when I felt a pain so sharp, it was like someone had stabbed me right in the centre of my chest. Moments later, I found our girls on the bathroom floor. I've thought about that over the years, and while there isn't any evidence for it, my belief is that when we are deeply connected, attuned to those we love, we feel it when they are no longer physically present—we 'know' when they no longer have life. I've heard many people say of a loved one who is thought to have died in an accident, they don't believe that person has died because they would feel it if it were true.

We don't do well at grieving and death in our society. After our girls died, I was lost. I agree with C. S. Lewis, who lamented, '*No one ever told me that grief felt so like fear. I am not afraid, but the sensation is like being afraid.*' I hadn't yet started writing, and I didn't know what to do with the anxiety and fear that continually dogged me. I needed to go deep within myself, to the very heart of me, where I was trying to deal with letting go, but it was too hard. I didn't want to let go. I didn't want it to be true. This deep part of us is the part that has been so deeply connected to the one we loved and if we go there, we have to admit that the connection as we knew it is broken, and the self, that part of us that loved and was connected to that person, has to change. I remember I didn't know who I was anymore.

When we are in that deep state of disconnection, it feels like we will die. But we won't. I talked earlier about the lost possible selves; from when we are children there are parts of us that we have to let go of, parts of us that will never be what we hoped they would be. Unless we let go of these selves, we can't grow and change as we need to; we can't fully engage in life as an adult.

The loss of self, together with the loss of someone dear to us, or something that was an integral part of our dreams and sense of purpose, can feel life-threatening. Our tendency, then, is to repress the healing process and stay in that place of pain and loss. We shut ourselves off from those around us, or our pain is so hard for others to see that they withdraw from us. Just when we most need the support and love of others, to feel that warm connection that is a part of healing, we spurn it, or it is withdrawn.

I was at a church function in 2002, so many years after our girls died, but running from facing my pain and allowing myself to grieve had driven me to push myself so hard in my career that I experienced burnout. I reluctantly agreed to attend the function and while there, I spoke with two ladies I had known since each of us was pregnant with our first child. They asked how I was. I told them—openly. I told them that I was struggling to move out of the house, that depression, which was one of the main symptoms of the burnout, was driving me to remain home, to hide away most of the time. Both said they would pray for me and committed to call to arrange a time to visit me. I was encouraged by that. I felt hopeful. In her book, *Braving the Wilderness*, author and researcher Brené Brown says that we all want to be part of something, but we need it to be real—not conditional or fake. We need true belonging. There was something in me that leapt at the thought of belonging again, of connecting. So, I waited. And waited. After a number of weeks, I decided they weren't going to visit me. The hope I had, left. Whether it would have made a difference, whether I would have recovered more quickly, I don't know. But believing that they cared enough to want to visit and to support me lifted my mood significantly. I thought we had connected in a meaningful way during our conversation that day. But real connection would have meant they at least called as they had promised.

I learned an important lesson through that time: I never promise something I can't or won't do. Doing so not only breaks connection, but it also breaks trust—and trust is not easily restored.

In grief, we don't always deliberately separate ourselves from others. We do it in subtle ways: emails go unanswered, the phone goes to voicemail, texts aren't responded to, we make excuses for not going out with our friends or going to special events. Sometimes our grief becomes about not being able to do things we used to do, or not being able to do things we dreamed of doing. Read Elizabeth's story again. One of the consequences of the choices she and her husband made was that they couldn't attend important family gatherings because they didn't have the money to buy plane tickets. This complicated the grief associated with those poor financial decisions. Many people can't relate to that sort of grief. It carries with it a sense of shame; shame that you were manipulated into something that could devastate your life in such a way. Guilt grows as you consider what others will think because you can't make it to the event. You can't explain because that would just add to the shame. Disconnection. It adds to the distress that is already intense. It adds to the pain of the loss, because it brings with it more loss.

'Bear one another's burdens.' This Bible verse, in Galatians 6:2, encourages us to be in community and to be connected to each other, no matter what is happening. Bearing one another's burdens isn't a fair-weather thing to do. Author and science journalist Daniel Goleman likens resonant relationships (relationships where there is a strong connection) to emotional vitamins. They sustain us through tough times and nourish us daily. When we are grieving, we need emotional vitamins more than ever. We need to be nourished daily. We need each other.

> 'Spirituality recognises and celebrates that we are all inextricably connected to each other by a power greater than all of us, and that our connection to that power and to one another is grounded in love and compassion.'
>
> Brené Brown, *The Gifts of Imperfection*

Connecting with Nature

The man who came to install our window made me laugh when he said he couldn't live where we do because it's too quiet. It is quiet, except for the birds. Early in the morning when I walk, there are no vehicles roaring around the roads. Often there is someone else, walking alone as I am or walking their dog. We greet each other and continue on our way. Trees line the paths I walk. There are birches, pines, Tuscan and other cypresses, and trees I love without knowing what they are. I stop in various places and gaze at the river far below, winding its way lazily from Launceston to the sea near Georgetown. I know the river has its problems but from up on the hill it gleams, even sparkles, in the light of a sun rising over the distant hills. Even when it's cloudy, the river is a reminder that life goes on, that even when there isn't a sparkle of sunshine or brightness in the sky, when the water appears a dull, muddy brown, it still does what it has always done. I arrive back home after a walk feeling calm, at peace and ready for whatever the day brings.

Over time, I've cultivated this ongoing connection with nature. I've even taken up bushwalking in the past few years, encouraged to do so by Jo, who has bipolar disorder. She was diagnosed a few years ago. Although we worked together many years ago, it wasn't until her spiral into despair pushed her into believing life was no longer worth living, that her family would be better off without her, that she could no longer stand the emotional and psychological pain she was in, that we connected again. I don't use the word 'connection' lightly but when we met there was an instant connection. We both knew our meeting was what some would call coincidence, but we felt it was divine intervention.

Jo was willing to do the hard work necessary to get to the bottom of the grief that was consuming her. It was a struggle because not only was she doing deep, very deep, emotional and psychological work but she was trying to find the right medication mix that would help her manage her bipolar. She needed something that would replenish her, refresh her and help her on the path to healing and personal growth that she was reaching for. Her mum and dad were bushwalkers, so getting out wasn't anything new to Jo, but she hadn't done any serious walking for a long while. Family and work commitments kept her busy, so there was never time for herself. Encouraged by her mum and dad, Jo started to get out in nature again.

In her book, *The Nature Fix*, Florence Williams writes of a number of recent studies that provide evidence of the many benefits to connecting with nature. I think one of the most interesting findings is that even brief immersion in nature can have a powerful effect on our emotions. Being in nature, even viewing nature videos, seems to trigger positive emotions in us—especially awe, wonder, gratitude and reverence. I often hear my son-in-law exclaim about the 'awesome' sights he sees during the outdoors adventures he and my daughter love to embark on. For Jo, getting out, bushwalking into remote places through challenging, and sometimes almost hostile terrain, became as essential as the medication she takes to stay well. One time I asked her what the most effective thing was that she was doing to remain stable. Her response was immediate, 'Bushwalking. It keeps me sane!'

Not everyone can bushwalk, but everyone can get outside even for a few minutes a day. I encourage all my clients to try it, and those who do always report back favourably. They also notice the drop in mood when they slip back into staying indoors, getting on the computer, or watching television rather than prioritising being outdoors.

Walking outside gives the opportunity to think about things in a reflective way. As we connect to nature, we open up to connecting with others—and to ourselves. Being in nature can help us develop a greater sense of connection to something so much bigger than ourselves and that can make our concerns seem, well, not as significant as we thought. It helps us with perspective.

When we are walking the grief path, we can become so narrow focused that we see little further than the step immediately in front of us. It's hard to lift our head and look beyond what is right now. The effect of being in nature can mitigate that. It causes us to look up, look around and look ahead. When we do that, we begin to see that the path ahead is not the same as the tiny bit we are on at any one moment. Just as it did for Jo, and has done for me too, being in nature, connected to nature, can give you hope.

Chapter 19

The Power of Emotion

>———————————————◄

Keeping ourselves in the picture in the midst of emotional chaos is the first step to finding a solution. That's not easy to do. When we are in the grip of strong emotions, our focus narrows to what is in front of our noses, not what's behind them: 'That's a problem,' 'He's a pain.' We're unable to give ourselves the loving attention we need.

Christopher Germer

Each of us has personal vulnerabilities that crop up when things are tough. When we don't recognise those tender spots, they can wreak havoc in our lives. For example, consider Elizabeth's story. If having made an unwise financial decision Elizabeth begins to see herself as a failure, then coping with being a 'failure', and choosing to live in the failure of the moment may lead to ongoing difficulties and inappropriate emotional behaviour. Psychologist and professor Paul Ekman says this can cause us to have a biased perception of the world and of ourselves. Being stuck in that space means Elizabeth's thinking can't incorporate information that doesn't fit, maintain, or justify the emotion she is feeling. This, in turn, makes finding ways to mitigate the damage of the financial decision a huge challenge; and this leads to ongoing feelings of failure.

As I write this, our world has been in pandemic mode for over a year. Many of us are stressed and worried wondering if it will ever end, and whether we will ever go back to pre-pandemic life. You may have suffered a lot of pain through the past year, pain you never imagined possible before the pandemic. I know people, and you may too, who have lost their business, who weren't able to attend the funeral of a loved one, whose children suffered academically because they couldn't go to school, or emotionally because of the social disconnection that occurred through not being allowed to socialise face to face in a physical way. And you may know someone who has been impacted by suicide in the past year. Emotions have often been in control rather than being controlled and it hasn't always been good.

I watched amazed as anger- and-rage-fuelled riots devastated towns and cities; as they destroyed businesses and lives while declaring their 'right' to be angry, their 'right' to express that anger even when it meant others would be harmed, or even killed. That's not emotional wellbeing, and it's definitely not emotional intelligence.

Emotional wellbeing doesn't mean being happy all the time. Although most of us prefer to feel positive emotions such as happiness, difficult emotions are a part of being human. We can't get rid of them, but we can learn how to manage them so that the sort of thing we saw happening during 2020 doesn't have to happen again.

Our emotional state, whether positive or negative, affects others. Anger, resentment, frustration and rage are sparks that ignite combustible material and start a conflagration that burns everything in its path. When allowed to run wild, negative emotions are just as destructive.

What does this have to do with grief? Below is a list of normal grief reactions. Note the feelings commonly felt by someone who is grieving.

Normal Grief Reactions

Feelings

- Sadness
- Anger
- Guilt
- Self-reproach
- Anxiety
- Loneliness
- Shock
- Fatigue
- Helplessness
- Yearning
- Emancipation
- Relief
- Numbness (depression)

Physical

- Hollowness in stomach
- Tightness in chest, throat
- Weakness in muscles
- Dry mouth
- Lack of energy
- Oversensitivity to noise
- A sense of depersonalisation (nothing seems real, not even self)

Cognitive

- Disbelief
- Confusion
- Preoccupation
- Hallucinations
- Sense of presence

Behaviour

- Crying
- Social withdrawal
- Absent-mindedness
- Dreams of the deceased
- Calling out and searching
- Sighing
- Avoiding reminders of the deceased
- Sleep and/or appetite disturbances
- Restless overactivity
- Carrying objects of the deceased or visiting places that remind the survivor of the deceased
- Treasuring objects that belonged to the deceased

We expect to see sadness at the top of the list. No matter the cause of our grief, sadness is always present, although it may be so inextricably mixed with other emotions that it isn't always obvious. Anger is close to the top of the list because it is often present in grief in some form. Like sadness, anger might not always be obvious as it can hide behind other emotions, or we push it down, suppress it, because we feel guilty about being angry. Fear is another feeling that is frequently present in grief.

The difficult emotions mentioned above are a natural part of grieving, but if they persist, they are often important signals alerting us to something going on internally. If we habitually attempt to suppress, avoid, or ignore emotional suffering, it can lead to more serious mental health issues such as anxiety and depression, and to physical illnesses according to the physician Gabor Maté, such as heart disease, diabetes, irritable bowel syndrome, multiple sclerosis, arthritis, and cancer.

James Pennebaker's psychological studies into the benefits of expressive writing opened the door for challenges to what has often been societal encouragement of inhibition—of holding back, or in some way exerting effort not to think, feel or behave as we need to in the face of trauma and other significant events in our life. The outcomes of Pennebaker's research confirm Maté's results—when we suppress, avoid, or attempt to ignore difficult emotions that arise from challenging life experiences our health suffers. The work of inhibition becomes a cumulative stressor on the body and mind; the harder we work at suppressing or avoiding our emotions, the greater the stress on the body.

We live in a world that tells us we should put on a happy face and look at everything through a positive lens. 'Don't worry, be happy' is a well-known mantra. We also know that whingeing and complaining alienates others and keeps us stuck in a negative place. Pennebaker suggests we confront trauma and the negative emotions associated with it. Events that lead to grief are often traumatic in some way. If we have an awareness of the emotions that are a normal part of the grief experience, and if we can accept them, can continue to confront them through talking, and or, writing about them it leads to developing that coherent story and, according to Pennebaker, a resolution of the trauma. This results in a lowering of the overall level of stress on the body and mind.

Years ago, when I first started offering expressive writing workshops, I was asked to facilitate one for a group of amazing people who were carers although not necessarily by choice. At the time, I was still learning about the power of writing and how deeply it can tap into our subconscious. It's a powerful therapy. We were on our second prompt, a simple list, when one of the participants let out a guttural scream and bolted out the door. I wasn't sure what to do and moved to follow her when an older woman put her hand on my arm and said she would go. We continued with the writing and after, as a group, talking about the activity and their responses we moved to another prompt. I was distracted as I was a little concerned about the woman who still hadn't returned, although not overly so as the other woman remained with her.

I heard a door bang and turned to see if the two ladies were returning, when there came a shout from another woman in the group.

'Gahhh! Now I know why I am so angry!'

I swung back in time to see her toss her pen down and burst into tears. The others remained in their seats and glanced at me. I felt it was important to let—I'll call her Mandy—cry until she decided it was time to stop so I quietly pushed a box of tissues along the table, although she didn't take any. She sobbed into her hands and I watched as the tears leaked through her fingers and plopped onto her notebook. I motioned to the others to continue with their writing and moved amongst them, glancing now and then at Mandy to make sure she was okay. Eventually she grabbed a few tissues, wiped her eyes, and blew her nose, then called my name. As she did, the door opened, and the other ladies returned. One nodded at me before taking her seat. I assumed that meant all was well, so turned my attention back to Mandy.

'Are you okay, Mandy?'

She nodded and asked if she could talk about what had happened. I was relieved Mandy had offered to share what was going on for her as I didn't want to intrude if she still needed to process it all.

Mandy then told the story of having to care for her grandchildren because her daughter wasn't able to. That wasn't what made her angry though. She had relied on her husband to help with the children and with everything else around the house. It was hard work being a grandmother, working part time and caring for two children whose lives had been upended by their mother's behaviour. For a while, things were working out, then her husband had a stroke. The writing prompt I had given the women brought to the surface all the feelings Mandy had been bottling up, unwilling to face since her husband had the stroke. There was anger at the position she was now in, helplessness because she had no control over what happened, fear because she was afraid she wouldn't be able to do all that was being demanded of her— she was beginning to feel overwhelmed; a sense of deep grief rising within her as the plans she and her husband had for their retirement could no longer be realised; guilt because she knew her husband had struggled with caring for their grandchildren and battled with his own anger towards their daughter.

While Mandy's story seems tragic, and in many ways it was, the writing workshop represented a new beginning for her. She began to write her story. As she wrote, she told me some months later, she felt a shift in perspective, a shift in her feelings, so that she was no longer stuck in the negatives. She spoke for a while about how she came to see she carried resentment towards her husband and as she worked on this in her writing, she traced that back to feeling abandoned by him. She shook her head as she shared, saying she had chosen to share this with her husband, and when she did, he grabbed her hands and cried with her as she asked his forgiveness. It wasn't easy for Mandy to travel the grief path through the losses she listed that day in the workshop, but each time she felt like giving up, she made an intentional choice not to. Each time she pushed forward she felt stronger she said, and while things hadn't changed much, she had, and she felt more able to cope well with what her life was. She was more aware of her emotions and no longer responded automatically; she was learning to sense the impulse before it led to action, to pause and reflect on what she was feeling and then choose how she would respond. It was an amazing shift for her.

Brené Brown says:

> 'You can't numb these hard feelings without numbing all of our emotions. You cannot selectively numb emotion. So, when we numb those hard feelings, we numb joy, we numb gratitude, we numb happiness.'

As for the other woman, she didn't write more in the workshop, but she did join in the discussions and had some greatly insightful comments to offer. After the workshop she told me she had dyslexia and had never really learned to write well—but she did attempt the list. Even before she managed to get anything on paper, she said, her head was full of things that were distressing her, things she had no idea how to change. Joining in with the others had been helpful, but the most helpful thing for her was realising she wasn't alone in her struggles. She said the sense of connection was amazing and it gave her hope that things could get better.

When I work with clients, helping them write their story, one of the areas that comes up often is regret. Jeff Bezos of Amazon fame developed what he called The Regret Minimisation Framework. It seems like a big title for what is essentially, making sure you don't leave undone something that you know, in ten years' time, you will regret not doing. It was this thinking that made him choose to leave a well-paying job to start up an Internet company with only a 30 percent chance of it succeeding. The framework, he said, made it incredibly easy: *'So I wanted to project myself forward to age 80 and say, Okay, looking back on my life, I want to have minimised the number of regrets I have.'*

Some of the regrets I hear are: *'I wish I had told him/ her, how I felt.' 'If only I had asked someone for help.' 'I am so sorry I didn't…' 'I am so sorry I did…'* A big regret for many that crops up time and again is not expressing their true feelings, but perhaps the most common is not having the courage to live their life and instead living as others expect them to. I remember hearing an interview with Bronnie Ware who wrote *The Top Five Regrets of the Dying* and nodding along as she spoke about the same regrets I was hearing from many of my clients. The thing with my clients though is that they have time to change their story—those Bronnie talked about never did get the chance to do that.

Cambridge Dictionary defines regret as, *'a feeling of sadness about something sad or wrong or about a mistake that you have made, and a wish that it could have been different and better.'*

The grieving process as mentioned above can bring to the surface feelings such as regret. Don't be like the many who were dying that Bronnie Ware interviewed. You have time to do something about the regrets and other big feelings that can be hard and painful to face. Be brave. Be honest about what you are feeling and choose to express not suppress them. Look back at Amelia's story. She speaks of a coin with two sides. On one side is the word 'regret' and on the other, 'hope.' Hope is a powerful driver for wellness. If you choose to see it as an option to living in regret, you will notice, that at times, it is the main motivation for continuing to move forward on your grief journey.

I don't know where the following quote is from, but I decided I did not want it to be true for me.

'I lived with crushing regrets because I was never brave enough to claim what I wanted.'

Chapter 20

The Power of
Self-Compassion

◆——————————◆

What is this self inside us, this silent observer,
Severe and speechless critic, who can terrorize us
and urge us on to futile activity
And in the end, judge us still more severely
For the errors into which our own reproaches drove us?
T.S. Eliot, *The Elder Statesman*

When grief visits us, the last thing we want to do is lean into it. Grief isn't a welcome visitor. And, just as we do with unpleasant people, we tend to avoid. What I've learned though, is that avoiding just brings more pain. Whether we like it or not grief will have its day. Grief is necessary. It is, despite us earnestly wishing it weren't, a part of life on this earth. All, or many, of the unpleasant emotions mentioned in the list in the previous chapter will show up at some time no matter the reason for our grief.

I mentioned earlier that we need to lean into our problems, lean into the difficulties and struggles; that means accepting the emotions that accompany those challenges. Accepting is not only about not avoiding, but also about not getting caught up in them, or exaggerating them. That's hard, especially when we are being told, by ourselves and others, that we need to be strong, we need to put it (whatever it is) behind us and get on with life.

A good friend recounted the story of overhearing two teenage girls on a bus one day. She was distraught as she told me that one of the girls loudly boasted of having had sex with all the boys at the party they attended the night before. She did it, it appeared, because her boyfriend broke up with her and she wanted to show him she didn't care, that she didn't need him.

'I was sitting in front of them,' my friend said, 'and I wished I had my headphones with me. It felt intrusive, even though they weren't being quiet. It was all I could do not to turn around and tell them there was a better way of dealing with pain.'

Too often I hear of emotionally wounded people choosing further emotionally wounding ways of coping. And coping is usually avoidance of the emotions that cry out for recognition. Although she may not have been aware of it, the teen who seemed to be boasting about her sexual conquests and about proving to the boyfriend who dumped her that someone else wanted her, most likely had the feelings of inadequacy and inferiority pushing her to what was an act of self-harm. Feelings of insecurity, of not being enough, cause us to make bad decisions and they definitely make us unhappy. Unless faced, leaned into, explored and accepted, the self-judgement that is present in uncertainty can get much worse.

All of us want to feel accepted and worthy; the struggle can be unrelenting. We put so much time into this, into ensuring we meet others' expectations, into caring about what others think of us that often the result is we feel angry, resentful, fearful. We try so hard to be perfect because we believe if we are perfect, we will be acceptable. I spent many years unknowingly attempting to prove to Mum that I was worthy, wanting her to show me she accepted me—even after she died. When our girls died the evidence of what I had been unknowingly carrying came to the surface in full force. Before they died, the anger, resentment and fear manifested in how I lashed out, screaming at the children and at my husband for no good reason, making a cutting, hurtful comment at times to a friend or colleague. After they died, I was overwhelmed with a sense of being punished, of failing as a mother. I told myself that because I hadn't met the expectations God had of me when he gave me our girls, he took them from me. I'd never felt quite good enough for my husband either, and I was so sure his family continued to wish he had married someone else. I didn't see myself as trying to be perfect, I thought I was doing what everyone did—striving to be my best, but there is a big difference between striving to be your best and trying to be perfect.

Brené Brown, in *The Gifts of Imperfection*, says perfectionism is a heavy shield we lug around thinking it will protect us. We use it to 'minimise or avoid the pain of blame, judgement, and shame'. I was trying to earn approval and acceptance by pleasing people and God, by performing, especially after our girls died when I threw myself into my career. I worked hard at being perfect and I was my harshest critic if I didn't get High Distinctions in my studies. The rejection of my childhood was always a part of my life and it tortured me after the girls died. Shame and guilt were strong and the tape that had played in my head for so many years on and off, 'there's something wrong with you' switched to continual play. My response was to hide how I really felt, to throw myself into building my nursing career, and to continue to be a 'good' Christian. But, of course, I could never achieve perfection, and this just intensified the pain and in turn I intensified my efforts to be perfect, while all the while I was losing myself.

Grief can bring a lot of things to the surface that have been hiding away deep inside us. They impact how we think, behave and react, but we aren't aware of what is driving us to respond the way we do—until grief forces us to acknowledge their presence. When that happens some of us will refuse to take the opportunity offered to change our story from that moment and will turn back to what is known. Although it sounds odd to say, there is comfort in the uncomfortable because it is a known, and it's not unusual to stay in a hard place because its predictable. Others of us will choose to step onto the unknown path.

Stepping onto an unknown path is like starting a new chapter in your story. You have a fresh, clean page to begin writing on. Once I decided to step onto the path, to make my first mark on that blank page, I had to think about what I wanted to fill the pages with and I knew it wasn't the toxic negativity, the fear that had almost crippled me for much of my life, fear that I would never measure up—in people's eyes, or for God. I didn't want to keep so much of myself from my husband anymore because I feared the rejection I might see in his eyes if he really knew me. I sat, pen poised above the page, for a long while.

I had been steadily and consistently reading a different version of the Bible, the Amplified Version, allowing myself to soak in the truth of God's Word when the words in Ephesians chapter one jumped out at me. They told me that God, in love, chose me before the beginning of time. I figured that when he chose me, he knew me, and all my faults, yet he still chose me. That gave me hope and I began to write about how I wanted my life to be.

Our continuous flow of thoughts is an involuntary process and although these thoughts are not always true—that's why I call some of them deceptive brain messages—they can shape our experiences and in turn our life. Some of what we might think of as true has been conditioned by past experiences until they become our core beliefs. I was finally seeing my thoughts for what they were.

It was around this time I attended a conference where Dr Jeffrey Schwarz was speaking. His talk was based on his book *You Are Not Your Brain*. He talked about how we can use our mind to retrain our brain so it doesn't constantly fill us with self-doubt and anxiety. I remember sitting forward in my seat when he said:

'Nothing is more confusing or painful than when your brain takes over your thoughts, attacks your self-worth, questions your abilities, overpowers you with cravings, or attempts to dictate your actions.'

Ha! I knew Dr Schwarz's talk was going to be a great help to me—not just for what I would learn to help my clients but for what I would learn to help myself. And it was. It was from Dr Schwarz I learned about deceptive brain messages. A deceptive brain message is 'any false or inaccurate thought or any unhelpful or distracting impulse, urge or desire that takes you away from your true goals and intentions in life (i.e., your true self)'. Well, I sure had been having a lot of those and the result was as Gandhi stated:

'Your beliefs become your thoughts,

Your thoughts become your words,

Your words become your actions,

Your actions become your habits,

Your habits become your values,

Your values become your destiny.'

I was already changing my story, but I had become a bit stuck. I was trying so hard and becoming more frustrated. It was a struggle to let go of who I thought I should be. That way of thinking had been with me for so long, but I was learning all the time, finding something new here and there. It was like a treasure hunt and I felt I was being led to the gems I needed one at a time. Like anything, it would have been too overwhelming if I had been confronted with everything I needed to do at once.

The next clue given to me was an invitation to do a seminar with Kristin Neff, a compassion researcher. Through her research she found that people who are compassionate toward their failings and imperfections have greater wellbeing than those who repeatedly judge and criticise themselves. I put this together with what I was beginning to believe about God, who is important in my life, and what I was learning about my brain, and hope grew stronger, although I realised I had no idea how to be compassionate toward myself. How do you become your own inner ally instead of an inner enemy?

Neff's seminar was informative and challenging. All the time I was listening to her I was thinking of clients who would benefit from self-compassion. We're not very good at doing that! When Neff asked if we would treat a friend the way we treat ourselves, I took notice. If a friend was feeling inadequate, or having a hard time, if they made a really bad decision would I tell them they were stupid or needy or being ridiculous? That they deserved whatever it was that was happening to them? I knew I wouldn't do that. If a friend was devastated because their partner or spouse, who they believed would be with them for a lifetime, walked out on them, would I tell them it was because they were hopeless and ugly and boring? Of course not. But strangely this is just the type of thing we say to ourselves—or worse. With self-compassion, we learn to speak to ourselves like a good friend.

Following the seminar, I went to the website and did the self-compassion quiz. I didn't score well. If you would like to do it, you will find the link in the resources section at the end of the book.

To better understand why self-compassion is so powerful, it helps to know what happens to us physiologically when we self-criticise. I had become really good at that in my attempts to be perfect. Essentially, when we criticise ourselves, we tap into our body's threat-defence system which perceives the criticism as danger or a threat. When the threat is perceived, our amygdala, which registers danger in the brain, is activated, releasing cortisol and adrenaline which causes our body to prepare to fight, flee or freeze. This system is great if there is a threat to our physical bodies but nowadays the threats we face are mostly psychological and relate to our sense of self or our self-image.

Feeling threatened puts a lot of stress on our mind and body. A short burst is manageable, but chronic stress can cause anxiety and depression. This is why habitual self-criticism is so bad for us—emotionally and physically. With self-criticism, we are both the attacker and the attacked, says Neff.

Let's explore the concept of self-compassion. If we are to allow ourselves to embrace who we are, who we've been created to be, then self-compassion is essential.

Self-Compassion

A moment of self-compassion can change your day. A string of such moments can change the course of your life.

Christopher K. Germer

According to Neff, self-compassion has three components: self-kindness, common humanity and mindfulness.

Self-kindness: being warm, gentle and understanding toward ourselves when we fail, suffer, or feel inadequate rather than ignoring the pain or beating ourselves up with harsh and critical words.

Common humanity: recognising that we are all connected, that we are all human and make mistakes and experience hardships on a regular basis—it's inevitable and not something that will happen to 'me' alone.

Mindfulness: taking a balanced approach to our pain, suffering and negative emotions so that we don't suppress or exaggerate our feelings. We cannot ignore our pain and feel compassion for it at the same time. Mindfulness requires that we don't over-identify with thoughts and feelings or get caught up and swept away by them.

It's important to note that being mindful and leaning into painful emotions means more than just not avoiding them. As already mentioned, it also means not exaggerating our feelings or over-identifying with them. When we do this, our feelings take over and control us rather than the other way around. For those of us who struggle with a need to be perfect, a need to meet the expectations (perceived or real) of everyone around us, this is key.

Here's an example.

Recently, I sent an email to a small group of people who are helping me with a project. Inadvertently, I used 'Cc' instead of 'Bcc'. The email was fairly generic, but it did thank them all for being a part of the project. The next day, one of the recipients emailed me to ask if I realised I had used Cc. She said she wasn't comfortable because another participant would see her name. She then expressed doubt about her contribution to the project.

I went into what Brown calls perfection paralysis. *Oh no! How could I do that? I was sure I had used Bcc. How stupid was I to think I could coordinate something like this if I can't even do the right thing with an email? What will the others think? What it they are upset too?* And on it went—until I caught myself and noticed I had been totally caught up in that negative reactivity, even to the point of feeling anxious. Then I looked at the title of this chapter, and I shook my head, and smiled. *Self-compassion, Karen. Be kind to yourself. This is not the end of the world.*

Later, my friend, Jo and I were talking generally about life one day, and I commented that she really wasn't very kind to herself.

'You need to practise self-compassion,' I said.

She snorted as only Jo can, 'As if!'

It was a completely foreign and unthinkable concept to Jo who had for so long been her own harshest critic—just as I was.

I mentioned earlier that grief can bring up some pretty unpleasant things for us. That's okay. But when that happens, stop for a minute, and ask yourself if you want to stay there, or do you want to move forward? Do you want to write 'The End' on your life story now, or is there more to come? When we are kind to ourselves, compassion can flow from us to others. Our children learn compassion by observing us, and those around us feel free to be real, authentic, and connected. There is so much to be gained from self-compassion. It's powerful when we choose to be deliberate about practising it.

PART FOUR

THE POWER OF WRITING: WORDS THAT HEAL

Chapter 21

Writing Can Save Your Life

>———————————————<

To write about what is painful is to begin the work
of healing.

Pat Schneider, *How the Light Gets In*

When I was in sixth grade, I had a bad case of chickenpox. Lots
of nasty sores popped up all over my body, and it was the
hardest thing not to scratch every one of them. On a table specially
placed beside my bed, in a room I was happy to have to myself instead
of sharing with my not so friendly older sister was my only defence
against the constant itch of the vesicles, bottles of a pink, chalky liquid
called Calamine lotion and a roll of cotton wool. Beside the lotion
and easily within reach was a jug of water. A usually half-filled glass
stood guard next to what was most important (to me): a pile of books.

I was devouring everything written by the Brontë sisters at the time, so the pile consisted of all the Brontë books available from our local library and my very own copy of *Jane Eyre*, a hurry up and get-well gift from Mum. These items were essential, I insisted, and I would not rest if any one of them was missing. After a week or so two items were added to the essential-to-me clutter: a little fat square diary and six Faber-Castell sketching pencils in a grey, white, and black tin with a lid that clicked closed.

'You can't read all the time, you'll ruin your eyesight,' Mum growled as she tossed the diary and pencils on the bed. 'Draw something or write in the diary. I can't be going to the library every other day to get books for you.'

So, although Mum's intention was to stop me being a nuisance, she did me a very big favour that day. I couldn't draw, other than odd-looking stick figures so I wasn't about to waste my time on that; but I could write. I loved to write. Having chickenpox wasn't a trial at all for me. I got to stay in bed, have my meals provided and not have to wash or dry the dishes, read all I liked and, once the diary arrived, I got to write too, and I could do it day or night without being yelled at for having the light on, or for being inside when I should have been outside. Despite the annoying itch and occasionally feeling unwell, I happily lost myself either in the world of the Brontë sisters or in my very own world of the short stories I wrote each day. I wrote stories about a little girl who was afraid of the night and how she became brave enough to face what scared her.

My dislike of night-time started when I was about eleven, not long before I got chickenpox—perhaps because I became more aware of the tension between Mum and her partner, especially when payday rolled around. It was at night that the yelling happened, that the sounds of someone being slapped or things breaking made me slide under the covers and push my hands over my ears. And then, it was at night that Mum's partner started coming into my room when he thought I was asleep. He just stood there beside the bed. I was never asleep, and I worked hard to calm my rapid breathing, prayed furiously that God would stop my heart from beating out of my chest, and even more furiously that God would make him go away. So, when I had chickenpox, I was happy. The virus was like an invisible barrier to the dangers outside my bedroom. I was awake at night, and possibly contagious, so no one other than Mum came near me. It was like being on holiday for six weeks—from school and other things.

Writing, on and off, has remained with me from that eventful sixth grade year. I graduated from a diary to a journal, and after our girls, Sarah and Ileana, died in 1993, the journal became my therapist. Not initially, because initially I stopped writing. I was like a petulant child refusing to engage with any writing because I could not, would not do anything that I might find solace in. My girls were dead, I was alive. It wasn't right or fair. I was a bad mother. I must have been for God to take two of my children. Not one, as if that wouldn't have been bad enough, but two. It didn't make sense unless I was being punished.

If only I had taken pen to paper when I was thinking that way, many years of heartache, self-recrimination, deep guilt, and shame may have been curtailed much sooner than the thirteen years it took for me to open up and allow grief to have its way.

Writing has helped me heal. And it can help you too. In this book you've read stories; stories written in the midst of deep pain and loss, or early after the healing process started, and some written well after so that the reader feels, at times, that healing is almost complete. Writing has helped all those who tell their story in this book. Will you let it help you?

I didn't realise as I wrote my little stories that I was engaging in therapy. I'm grateful no one thought my scribblings were worth reading so I didn't have to worry about hiding what I wrote. When I think back to what found its way onto the page in thick, black graphite, perhaps

I should have been concerned. Years later, after our girls had died and after I reluctantly allowed grief to have its way, I realised how significant the writing was in those early years, in helping me to build resilience. I thought my family life was normal—until I started writing stories that shouted the truth at me:

'It's not normal to have an alcoholic mother. It's not normal to be ignored. It's not normal to fear your stepfather.'

As a child I didn't know what to do with the darkness that was a constant in my stories, so rather than let the stories unfold naturally, since it was always darkness that dominated, I began to plan. I at least wanted a happy ending and so instead of writing about what did happen, I wrote about what I wished would happen! In my own way, I was using writing as therapy.

A Sturdy Ladder

Alice Walker, author of the book, *The Colour Purple,* commented that writing for her, for all of us, 'is a matter of necessity and that you write to save your life is really true and so far, it's been a sturdy ladder out of the pit.'

Writing as a 'sturdy ladder out of a pit' is a great metaphor. Even though there is a pit, there is something safe, strong, and dependable that provides a way out. Writing has been a way to reach safety and freedom for those who have shared their stories in this book; for some it continues to be. When grief drags us into the pit, no matter how deep and dark it is, we can be sure that writing is always there to help us find the way out.

Writing Can Save Your Life

Although I had no idea how writing could be so helpful, all my reading—and I read widely, both research papers and books—and interactions with those who have used this kind of writing confirmed that writing can produce profoundly beneficial psychological and even physical effects. Eventually, I gave up trying to figure it out and simply accepted that in writing about upsetting events, about things that were painful and even devastating for me, I often came to a new understanding of the emotional events themselves. After I saw them on paper, the problems that seemed like undefeatable giants that kept my brain working overtime at night to try and figure out a solution somehow became more manageable. As I wrote about what happened to our daughters, about my problematic relationship with Mum, and about other past experiences that had haunted me, I noticed a change within myself. Writing helped me to make some sense of the horrible things that happened in my life; it didn't change what had happened, of course, but it did change how I viewed those haunting experiences. They no longer constantly intruded into my thinking. Alice found writing helpful too.

'Coming to this workshop, doing this writing has been so hard. I wanted to give up after the first prompt, but I didn't and I'm glad. I think this writing has saved my life!'

Alice almost cancelled her registration for the workshop a couple of times. I was seeing her to help her make sense of why her husband of three years would suddenly walk out. No explanation, no warning. Alice arrived home from work one day and found a note saying he'd gone, and she shouldn't try to contact him. Although she never did hear from him, she assumed he would file for divorce after the mandated waiting period. Alice started seeing me a few months after he left, when she was diagnosed with depression.

'I can't stop thinking about what he took with him when he went. He took part of me. He took the child we were going to have together; he took the future we planned. I don't know what to do with that.'

For a couple of years before I met Alice, I'd been reading about researcher Laura King's work. She explains that thinking about what might have been, ruminating on it as Alice was, or thinking about our lost possible self—what never was, almost was, no longer is—is a recipe for regret, deception, bitterness, humiliation, sadness (that can become depression) and anger. I shared this with Alice.

Alice was in that deep, dark pit of loss I mentioned earlier. She hadn't considered she might be grieving but as we talked about what her husband's abandonment meant to her emotionally, psychologically, physically and spiritually, Alice wept. She held herself tightly, wrapping her arms around her thin body and rocked back and forth, sometimes sobbing loudly, sometimes weeping silently. Eventually she calmed, leaned her head back on the chair and with eyes closed, sighed deeply.

'So, what do I do now?'

I wanted to show Alice that there was a ladder out of the pit she was in and so I suggested she write. I suggested she write a goodbye letter to the lost possible selves.

She did, and a few weeks later, Alice attended a *Grieving Your Way* writing workshop with me. After that, writing became a part of her daily routine and now and then I still hear from her. Although she isn't writing every day as she used to, there are times when she pulls out her journal and writes to make sense of what's going on for her in that moment. The best thing is that in saying goodbye to the lost possible selves as she did, Alice was not only able to make room for new possible selves, but she could also enjoy who she was in the present, and that continues.

In the next chapter you will find a few of the writing prompts that have helped so many of those I have worked with. Those I have chosen have been especially useful for clients seeking to find their way through unimaginable loss. One of the prompts is the letter to the lost possible self that Alice found instrumental in getting her out of the pit.

Writing *can* save your life! I know that sounds a bit dramatic, but many years after I first began to use this kind of writing to help me make some sense of the horrible things that had happened in my life, the evidence is mounting that writing has helped, and continues to help, people heal.

Whether it has saved my life or not, I can't be sure, but writing has helped me deal with my own health challenges, including anxiety and depression, and a diagnosis of invasive skin cancer. After reading Louise de Salvo's book, *Writing as a Way of Healing*, I searched for more information and more guidance in how to use expressive writing effectively. I read *Opening Up: The healing power of expressing emotions* by Professor James Pennebaker and what I read resonated with me. It made sense—especially for someone who had such difficulty expressing emotions in any way. Then I found Pennebaker's *Writing to heal: A guided journal*. I liked that this journal was grounded in scientific research, that there was evidence demonstrating this way of writing was helpful. During the years in which I refused to write in my journal, I was a teacher and student of academic writing, but that was not helpful to me personally and emotionally, so I hoped that the guided writing in *Writing to Heal* might be something that would help me write my way out of the grief and subsequent depression that seemed impossible to shift.

When the book arrived, I started reading immediately and found within just a few pages why the writing I had been doing was not helping. I was writing my story, but writing the same one over and over, and I was focusing on only negatives; it never went anywhere—a bit like *Groundhog Day*, if you have seen that movie. *Writing to Heal* was the beginning for me to reframe the narrative that I had in my head, to rewrite my story in a way I don't think I would have considered if I had not come across this book. Pennebaker's book guided me in rewriting or working through, not only the more recent traumatic events in my life, but also some of the childhood and adolescent troubling events and subsequent painful memories. I was able to lay to rest or bring closure to these and move beyond that memory induced emotional turmoil that I hadn't even realised was always close to the surface. It also helped me understand why I struggled so much with my faith and never felt 'enough' in any of my relationships, including that important spiritual relationship with God. Eventually, knowing the power of this kind of writing lead me to the Center for Journal Therapy and training with Kathleen Adams as a *Journal to the Self* instructor.

My memoir, *Healing Begins in the Heart*, was birthed from this different approach to journal writing that was helping me make sense of the huge losses I had experienced in my life. It was the writing that gently pushed me towards the grief and pain, to where I came to see it as something to be tended to and not avoided, or a problem to be solved. Writing my memoir didn't erase the grief I was carrying, but it did allow me to finally walk with Grief instead of continuing to run from it. In the writing, I felt I was honouring Grief as I opened up to it and learned what it wanted to tell me. I was finally able to say, 'I hurt. I hurt.' I didn't need to figure things out anymore or make excuses for why God allowed my girls to die that Saturday evening in Quito, Ecuador.

An Invitation

Since you are here, I'm assuming you are grieving, or you know someone who is, and you want to help them. I believe there is so much you can learn from this book that *will* help you; one of those things is the power of expressive writing when you choose to engage with the writing process. If you choose to engage, over time you will find you discover strength, greater insight into who you are and what is happening to you, wisdom, creativity, depth and even wholeness. So, I invite you to write, to choose to engage in the writing process, and see what happens. Below are a few more proven benefits of expressive writing:

- Immune system is enhanced
- People with chronic illnesses show improvement in their general health
- Physiological indicators of stress improve (such as blood pressure and heart rate variability)

- Reports of depressive symptoms, rumination and general anxiety tend to drop in the weeks and months after writing about emotional upheavals
- People report feeling happier and more positive
- People adjust better to changing situations
- Working memory is improved
- Social life quality can be enhanced.

You can read about the studies that demonstrate the above evidence in some of the books you will find in the reference list.

After each writing activity, write a reflection.

Read what you have written. Pay attention to what you notice, what surprises you, what stands out for you. Maybe something suddenly makes sense, or you remember something you forgot. Pay attention to your body: where does this write 'land' in you? When you finish reading, write a sentence or two about the writing process and what you noticed as you were writing. These reflection or feedback statements can be a source of great insight. They can open the way to finding meaning in what you have written and making connections, bringing the hidden parts of yourself into your consciousness.

Chapter 22

Writing Prompts

>────────────────────────<

Our own wounds can be vehicles for exploring our essential nature, revealing the deepest textures of our heart and soul, if only we will sit with them, open ourselves to the pain... without holding back, without blame.

Wayne Muller, *Legacy of the Heart*

A basic writing exercise advocated by Pennebaker and others is to write for twenty minutes each day for four consecutive days.

The Four Day Exercise

What is the loss that is uppermost in your mind; something that is extremely personal and important? When you have decided what it is, commit to writing about it for the next four days. By the fourth day, you will be able to stand back and reflect on what you have written—the issues, thoughts, and feelings you disclosed. Please be honest with yourself about the loss you have chosen to write about and how it has changed your life. On the fourth day, you should be able to write a coherent, meaningful story about your loss. Dan Siegel says that making sense of how experiences have affected us is a source of strength and resilience, and making sense (not blaming anyone, or trying to figure things out) is essential to our happiness and wellbeing. Author Wayne Muller says we need to stop trying to figure things out and simply acknowledge that it—whatever it is—happened, and because it happened, we hurt.

Some things to remember while you are writing:

Write for twenty minutes each day—it's okay if you write for longer but don't take that off the next day's twenty minutes! Each day, you write for at least twenty minutes.

Writing topic—write about the loss you have decided to focus on. You can write about it as a whole every day, or you can select a different aspect of the loss each day.

Write continuously—once you start writing, don't stop. Don't worry about spelling, grammar or sentence structure. Say the same thing over again if you run out of things to say. However you choose to write, just keep writing until the twenty minutes are up. Set a timer if that will help.

STOP—if it is too hard for you. If you feel writing about a particular loss will push you over the edge, then don't write about it. Choose something else and, when you are ready to write about that other loss, come back to it.

Write for yourself— this first exercise is for you. The purpose of the writing is not for it to be a letter to someone else, although it can be a letter to yourself.

'Trust your own instincts in your writing. If, after writing something, you feel as though you have gained benefit from it even though most other people would view it as a jumbled mess, then pat yourself on the back. You have succeeded.'

James Pennebaker,
Expressive Writing; Words that Heal

List your Losses and Structured Write

Loss and grief go hand-in-hand. One of the writing activities we do in the *Grieving Your Way* workshop is to list your losses. Writing lists is a great way to gather information—think of this exercise as gathering information on the losses you have experienced.

Stop now and take some time to list some of your own losses. See if you can list 5-10 things, no matter how seemingly big or small. It will take courage to actually identify your losses and you might be surprised at the cumulative effect these have on you. If you go back to Di's story of grief you will read about her reaction to the death of a baby plover. She recognised that it wasn't that particular loss that caused such an overwhelming emotional response. The death of the baby plover was one more loss on top of others that she seemingly took in her stride over the year before. Her response to what happened to the baby plover was the cumulative effect of all the losses.

As you list your losses you may find you have an emotional response; it may be tears, it may be anger. Allow the emotions to be there. They're there for a reason. If a strong emotion does surface, or you begin to feel overwhelmed, feel free to leave the list for now and begin what is called a Structured Write, focusing on the emotion that is demanding your attention.

Structured Write

This writing prompt is a variation on the Structured Write that Kathleen Adams uses in her book, *The Way of the Journal*.

1. Notice the time. You don't want to write for more than 10-15 minutes.

2. Ask yourself, 'How am I feeling right now?' Write the emotion (or emotions) at the top of your page.

3. Begin with: *As I was writing a list of the losses, I noticed anger (or whatever emotion you are working with) begin to bubble up inside me...* let whatever comes, come. Don't censor your own words, don't worry about punctuation or grammar. Just write.

4. At the end of the 10-15 minutes, sit with what you have written, then after a few minutes, reread it and note what stands out to you. Write this down.

5. Write down the emotion or feeling that is now most present for you.

You can do the Structured Write any time. Because it is contained timewise, it's especially helpful when you are overwhelmed in any way, or if you want to focus on just one thing, or even to track something that's concerning you over time.

Once you have completed your list of losses, you can choose to go to the website karenmace.com where you will find a workbook that contains, among other writing prompts, another list. If you like, compare yours and the one I have provided and see if there are any that apply to you.

1. List any additional losses.

2. Now list in order of priority those you plan to work through.

3. List the losses you no longer need to deal with.

4. Have you made any progress in working through your losses? Write about this.

Lost Possible Self

It's not easy to say goodbye to what might have been or to who we might have been but if we are to move forward, it's important to let go of plans that won't materialise or didn't materialise. The lost possible self is usually associated with an event that does not eventuate. It may be that you were sure you would marry and have children and that hasn't happened, so your dream of you as a wife, mother and grandmother won't be realised, and that self you saw in your dreams is lost. You may have dreamed and planned to be in a financially comfortable position by retirement, but this doesn't happen so the self you see at retirement is nothing like the self you envisioned, that self is lost, swept away with the dreams you had about how life would be at this time.

We are happier when we recognise and face our losses and our lost possible selves but are not consumed by them, when we focus on our best possible self now and even a best possible future self. When we think this way, we have hope, and when we hope, our wellbeing improves.

Letting go of the lost possible self requires opening yourself up to the pain associated with the loss, allowing yourself to grieve.

Goodbye Letter to Lost Possible Self

You can choose to write to one particular self, or to all the lost possible selves. Begin by writing down the selves you want to say goodbye to. Then begin to write:

Dear (name the lost possible self, or the event you won't experience if that is easier)

In your letter acknowledge her or him, thank the lost possible self for how it helped you, write about the feelings you have around letting go, and write, if you can, about how not becoming that self you thought you would be, has reshaped your life.

The Bridge

When people attend one of my writing workshops, I don't allocate seating; I allow them to sit wherever they like. From the very first writing prompt about listing your losses, on the day of my very first *Grieving Your Way* writing workshop, everyone at one particular table did some deep emotional work during the workshop. But I want to tell you about Sally, because the next writing prompt I am giving you is one that caused Sally to resist—strongly. The prompt is The Bridge, and it's one of the most powerful writing prompts I ask my clients to try. I have seen clients use it over and over, and each time they find it either brings a new revelation or breakthrough, or it causes great resistance, which in turn leads to an exploration of why they have put up this barrier. Sally absolutely refused to 'cross the bridge', but she left the workshop determined to face it. And she did. She went back again and again to The Bridge until one day, about six weeks after the workshop, I answered the phone to her shout of, 'I did it. I crossed the bridge!'

'And the fear?' I asked.

'Still there, but I faced it down and stepped onto the bridge anyway, and with each step the fear got smaller and smaller, so that by the time I got to the other side it was no more than a speck of dust.'

The laughter and joy in her voice had me smiling too. We chatted for a bit longer and I didn't see Sally again until just recently. I was as excited to hear, as she was excited to tell, of how crossing the bridge was freeing for her in many ways. It opened the door to connections she could never have made before, to forgiveness (of others and of herself) she thought would be impossible to access, and to letting go of aspects of herself that would never be realised—those lost possible selves that kept pulling her back to the past. She chose to write a goodbye letter to those lost possible selves, which she said was almost as hard as crossing the bridge. Sometimes one of those selves tries to get her attention, she said, but each time she reminds herself that while that self served her for a time, it no longer does, and so she is able to turn away without regret.

Here's The Bridge if you would like to try it. Remember, you don't have to cross the first time, but if you choose not to, if you find resistance is strong and you stop writing, then please come back to it at some point. I've not met anyone who has regretted doing The Bridge write.

The Bridge exercise involves these five steps:

1. You are standing at the edge of a narrow suspension bridge strung high above a dangerous drop to rocks and rushing water. You want to cross but you are concerned that there is no safety rail to prevent you from falling. You look back for a few seconds at what you are leaving behind. Briefly describe this and the feelings that arise as you consider what you are leaving behind.

2. Now, describe the bridge and your surroundings.

3. Write about why you want to cross and how you feel about it.

4. Look across to the other side of the bridge. Notice who is standing at the end to meet you. See them wave and call to you. Write about this and the effect it has on you.

5. Once you have developed the writing into a story and completed it, reflect on what you have written and summarise it.

List of Supports

1. Write a list of supports you have during this uncertain time. Include anything that might help you gain clarity and structure: friends, family, beliefs, exercise, pets, books, movies, gardening—they all count. Highlight those that seem most important to you *at the present moment*.

2. Write for at least five minutes about how you will take advantage of the most important supports.

3. Use this as a reminder to take care of yourself. You may decide to change the relative importance of each of your supports from time to time, and as you do, write another self-care exercise.

A Poem

When despair comes

When despair for the world

Overwhelms me

And I wake in the night

Afraid, fearing what tomorrow might hold

I go to my quiet place and lie down where the moon

Sends its light through the open shutters

And I can hear the leaves of the birch rustling in the wind

The sound of night animals crashing fearlessly in the dark

Reminds me they don't live with grief on their minds

And I remember the holy Scriptures and the promise of

A place of still, calm pools after the struggle through a wilderness

And I feel above me and around me the presence of light

And grace waiting for me to submit

To rest in the love that will hold me.

Karen Mace

PART FIVE

REFERENCES AND RESOURCES

Resources

EXPRESSIVE WRITING

If you are interested in learning more about expressive writing you might find the following resources helpful:

Adams, K. (1990). *Journal to the self: 22 Paths to personal growth.* New York, NY: Grand Central Publishing.

Adams, K. (1998). *The way of the journal* (2nd ed.). Arvada, CO: The Sidran Institute Press.

DeSalvo, L. (2000). *Writing as a way of healing: How telling our stories transforms our lives.* Boston, MA: Beacon Press.

Lepore, S. & Smyth, J (Eds). (2006). *The writing cure.* Washington, DC: American Psychological Association.

Pennebaker, J. W. (2004). *Writing to heal: A guided journal for recovering from trauma & emotional upheaval.* Oakland, CA: New Harbinger.

Pennebaker, J. W. (1990). *Opening Up: The healing power of expressing emotions.* New York, NY: The Guilford Press.

Pennebaker, J. W & Evans, John F. (2014). *Expressive writing: Words that heal.* Enumclaw, WA: Idyll Harbor Inc.

GENERAL

Attig, T. (2002). Disenfranchised grief revisited: Discounting hope and love. *OMEGA*, 49(3), 197-215.

Bradbury, Laura. (2020). *My grape Quebec.* Kindle Edition.

Brown, B. (2017). *Braving the wilderness: The quest for true belonging and the courage to stand alone.* London, UK: Penguin Random House.

Brown, B. (2010). *The gifts of imperfection.* Center City, MN: Hazelden.

Ekman, P. (2007). *Emotions revealed: Recognising faces and feelings to improve communication and emotional life. Paperback – Illustrated* (2nd ed.).

Germer, C. K. (2009) *The mindful path to self-compassion: Freeing yourself from destructive thoughts and emotions.* New York, NY: The Guilford Press.

Lewis, C.S. (2012). *The problem of pain.* London, UK: William Collins.

Lewis, C.S. (1961). *A grief observed: Reader's edition.* London, UK: Faber and Faber.

Mace, K. A. (2014). *Healing begins in the heart: Snapshots of God's transforming work—looking back, moving forward.* Available from karenmace.com/Healing Begins in the Heart.

Maté, G. (2011). *When the body says no: Exploring the stress-disease connection.* Hoboken, NJ: John Wiley & Sons.

Muller, W. (2012) *Legacy of the heart: The spiritual advantages of painful childhood* (eBook).

Neff, K (2011). *Self-compassion.* New York, NY: Harper Collins.

Neff, K & Germer, C. (2018). *The mindful self-compassion workbook.* New York, NY: The Guilford Press.

Palmer, P. J. (2000). *Let your life speak: Listening for the voice of vocation.* San Francisco, CA: Jossey-Bass.

Pape, Scott. (2017). *The barefoot investor*. Milton, Australia: John Wiley & Sons.

Ratey, J. & Hagerman, E. (2008). *Spark: How exercise will improve the performance of your brain*. London, UK: Quercus.

Schwarz, J.M. & Gladding, R. (2012*). You are not your brain*. New York, NY: The Penguin Group.

Williams, F. (2017). *The nature fix*. New York, NY: W. W. Norton & Company, Inc.

LINKS

Dilruba Ahmed, 2020. Phase One.

https://onbeing.org/poetry/phase-one/

Self-compassion resources and the self-compassion quiz

https://self-compassion.org/

Romm, Cari. Understanding how grief weakens the body

https://www.theatlantic.com/health/archive/2014/09/understanding-how-grief-weakens-the-body/380006/

Shelley Whizen, 2018. Uniqueness of grief: A perspective on understanding disenfranchised grief (lovelifeandbeyond.com)

Bobbi Emel, 2021. Financial loss and grief

https://thebounceblog.com/articles/bouncing-back-from-financial-grief-and-loss/

The Conversation. The seriousness of financial loss.

https://theconversation.com/losing-wealth-health-and-life-how-financial-loss-can-have-catastrophic-effects-93639

ORGANISATIONS

New Mornings – A Christian, non-profit, community-based mental health support organisation based in Ulverstone, North West Tasmania. They offer a Grief and Loss Support Programme which commenced in April 2021.
www.newmornings.org.au

Australian Centre for Grief and Bereavement (ACGB)
(03) 9265 22100
https://www.grief.org.au

FREE WORKBOOK

A Grief Revealed Workbook available at karenmace.com/workbook

Gratitudes

It's taken me a long time to write this, my second book. Special thanks to my friend, Julie Sladden. Without her daring to tell me my 'thing' was grief, I may never have considered it. Pen Beeston thank you for sharing your artistic and creative talent with me through many brainstorming sessions. To all those who contributed their story to this book, thank you.

Special thanks to my patient and always-encouraging husband who never minds if the evening meal is eggs on toast because I have been busy writing!

And to the many others who are always there to pray and encourage—thank you.

About the Author

———————————————

Karen A. Mace is the author of the memoir, *Healing Begins in the Heart,* and its companion workbook, along with the expressive writing programme, *Your Brain on Paper.* A counsellor and journal therapist by day and an aspiring novelist and writer by night, Karen has qualifications and experience in nursing, education, counselling and psychology and brings elements of each to her writing, as well as her Christian faith, which is foundational to her work. In addition to seeing clients individually, Karen runs writing workshops, including her popular Grieving Your Way workshop, where participants learn to use expressive writing to work through their personal challenges and difficulties. Born in Melbourne, Australia, Karen considers herself a native of Tasmania where she has lived for most of her life, except for the years she and her family spent in Costa Rica and Ecuador. She and her husband live in Grindelwald, Tasmania, in an idyllic location perfect for both therapy and writing!

You can visit Karen online at karenmace.com and chat with her on Instagram at @karenmacewriter or on Facebook at @karenmacewriter.

KAREN A MACE

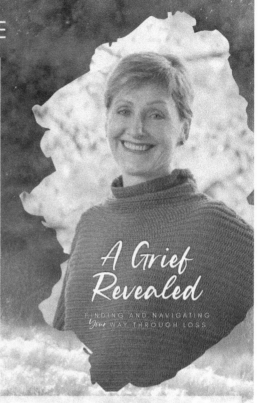

During her years as a Registered Nurse and as a Registered Counsellor, and through her own experience with grief, anxiety, depression and burnout, Karen Mace has learned that it is not sustainable to keep on giving without caring for self. Living well comes through knowing ourselves, our strengths and values, and trusting ourselves to live true to who we really are.

Karen understands that the key to a great presentation is an engaging delivery. She captivates her audience with her warm conversational style and inspires with her insight, stories, authenticity, and strength. Karen has a way of weaving stories and practical examples to leave her listeners with a take home message to facilitate learning and growth.

As a nurse, counsellor, educator and author, Karen has dedicated her life to helping others. Her personal experience of navigating grief and loss equips her to do this. Karen's work focuses on wellness, healing and hope. From small group workshops to a full auditorium keynote, your presentation will be tailored to the interests of your audience to offer a presentation that is interesting, engaging, and a stimulus for change.

✓ GRIEVING YOUR WAY
The changing face of grief
How to make grief your friend
Leaning in and pushing through the hard times

✓ STRESS and GRIEF
Understanding how stress and grief work together
How to recognise toxic stress
How to recognise the difference between grief and depression
Key strategies to minimise and eliminate toxic stress

✓ 7 STEPS TO AN ABUNDANT LIFE
How to open yourself up to receiving good things from others and from God
The secrets to bringing your life into balance
How to turn off the critical inner voice and listen to the truth about who you really are

DYNAMIC SPEAKER

STRENGTHS COACH

COUNSELLOR & JOURNAL THERAPIST

ACCOMPLISHED AUTHOR

INSPIRING STORYTELLER

To enquire about engaging Karen to speak at your next event, email **info@karenmace.com** *for prices and availability. Fees may be waived for NFPs.*

Notes

Notes

CPSIA information can be obtained
at www.ICGtesting.com
Printed in the USA
JSHW031036080721
16706JS00002B/124